FAIRY TALES

To Marion — thank
you for your interest
and it was lovely to
chat to you on the
phone!
I hope you enjoy
reading this as much as I
enjoyed writing it!

John

2nd Edition
published in 2011 by

Woodfield Publishing Ltd
Bognor Regis PO21 5EL England
www.woodfieldpublishing.co.uk

© John McGregor, 2010, 2011

ISBN 1-84683-109-1

Printed and bound in England
Last revised ~ 21 July 2011

Cover design by Mike Rowland FRCBS

Fairy Tales of an SAC

*A Young Airman's Experiences in
the Royal Air Force 1967-72*

JOHN MCGREGOR

Woodfield

Woodfield Publishing Ltd

Bognor Regis ~ West Sussex ~ England ~ PO21 5EL
tel 01243 821234 ~ **e/m** info@woodfieldpublishing.co.uk

Interesting and informative books on a variety of subjects

For full details of all our published titles, visit our website at
www.woodfieldpublishing.co.uk

This book is dedicated to my family, the rock on which I built my life; and especially to my late, wonderful parents, Lucy and Jack McGregor.

Through Toil to the Cinema.[1]

---

[1] Every large RAF station has its own cinema, usually called the 'Astra'. *Per Ardua ad Astra* is the RAF motto, meaning 'Through Toil to the Skies' but known jokingly within the RAF as the above!

~ CONTENTS ~

The Author

John McGregor was born in Bedford in 1949, the son of a New Zealand father and English mother, and has two sisters and a brother. He went to several schools in the south of England before his family settled down in Nottingham in 1958. Nottingham Forest won the FA Cup in 1959 and John became an ardent fan, 'BC' (Before Cloughie!). He went to High Pavement Grammar School in 1960, where he was taught English for two years by the author Stanley Middleton. John joined the Royal Air Force in 1967 as an aircraft radio technician and travelled the world extensively. After his five years' service he left the RAF and in 1972 joined Nicholas Products Limited as a Junior Salesman, to embark on a selling career that spanned twenty-six years and took him to senior sales positions with four different companies. John moved with the jobs and has lived in Wrexham, Swindon, Thatcham, Dunstable, Tring and Northampton.

Following a ten-year obsession born from his company's first sponsorship in 1980, John ran the London Marathon in 1990.

In 1995 he bought a house in Spain with a view to taking an early retirement but spends time between England and Spain as he follows his various hobbies. These include finishing off his education by studying for a degree in English at the Open University, writing, travel, seeing his family, playing his guitar badly and counselling work. John lives with his wife Anne and boss(y) cat Cleo, and has two children and four grandchildren.

Acknowledgements

I would like to acknowledge the unswerving love, help and devotion of my wife Anne in encouraging me to write this book. She recently told me that when she first met me and I said I was going to write a book about my time in the RAF one day, she didn't really think I meant it – but she has supported me all the way.

John Riddle was the first publisher who encouraged me, telling me I could write in an entertaining fashion and who first published a story I had written in his magazine. I would also like to thank the author Nik Morton for his valuable help and support with my writing, encouraging me to join a writers group and, last but not least, Nick Shepperd from Woodfield Publishing, who has been such a valuable mentor in guiding me through the publishing process.

Introduction

The five years I spent in the Royal Air Force in the latter half of the sixties and early seventies were some of the funniest and most enjoyable of my life and changed me forever. The big wide world was also changing, although the RAF was slow to respond but I soon became accustomed to its quirky ways and it became second nature over the five years I served her Majesty. But I was at an impressionable age and much of what happened inside and outside the Royal Air Force Station in that period stuck with me. I will never forget the young men and women I knew at the time and over the ensuing years I wrote most of these stories in my head long before committing them to paper.

I still have one good friend from that era today, my best mate in life, who features heavily and regularly in this book. He tells me I have a very good memory to be able to recall some of the events but he has also prompted my recall on several occasions about what happened to us during those far-off days. On the subject of memory, I quote that great aged rocker Ozzy Osborne: 'I can remember what happened forty years ago like it was yesterday. The trouble is trying to remember what *did* f***ing happen yesterday!'

I know exactly what he means...

All good things come to an end and I left the RAF to re-join that still-changing world outside the armed forces, where I soon got on with the job of re-learning about civilian life, with its new responsibilities of marriage, raising children, mortgages and career progressions in my chosen field, but I always wondered if one day I could write down what I remembered, to try to recapture in print those heady days. There wasn't time in my thirties, forties or fifties but as I approached sixty and life's busy pace began to slacken, I resolved to do it. I eventually sat down and tackled the job over six months in 2009 – and have succeeded, as you can see.

Better late than never, eh?

1. Leavin' on a Jet Plane

I opened my eyes. I was lying naked on my side in a big, comfortable bed in a strange room. The sight of my girlfriend Jill's nude bum swam into view close alongside me. The pleasing view of her ample, marbled, Botticelli curves transmitted their signal directly to the dormant aerial in my groin and nature began to take its course in my testosterone-laden nineteen-year-old body. However, all was not well elsewhere; other issues were attempting to force feed urgent information to my brain to alter its desirable viewpoint. The random order crowding in included: a hangover (a savage headache was increasing, obviously far too much alcohol consumed); the nurses' housewarming party last night; a hazy bragged intention to christen our now-occupied double bed; and lastly, but easily most importantly – OH MY GOD! – I was due to take off on detachment to Cyprus on the first aircraft of four that morning ... at seven o'clock.

Grabbing my watch it read – six o'clock! Her Majesty was calling me urgently. At that time, July 1969, I was a serving airman in the Royal Air Force, stationed at Thorney Island near Portsmouth on the South Coast of England. I jumped out of bed to see my previous night's party clothes strewn round the room. My new yellowish floral shirt with the cool penny round collar was masquerading as a floor mat but I urgently threw that, and what else I could find of mine, on. There was a suspicious sickly smell and one or two unsightly stains on the shirt, which I chose to ignore under the pressing business of rushing to serve my Queen and country.

I shouted to Jill that I would phone (from inside the guardhouse, presumably) and stumbled downstairs. In the hallway I passed the open door of the lounge, only to observe one my mates, 'Spanner' Harris, curled up peacefully like a dog on the lounge carpet. Spanner was also on the detachment but was on the last aircraft out. I now sincerely wished that I was. Grabbing him by the scruff of his neck, I hauled him out to my beloved little old banger of a car, a grey Austin A30 known affectionately as 'The Pig' (due to its registration number PYG 640).

Our eight-mile journey along the A27 would take about twenty minutes, giving me just enough time to make the flight, although it would be very tight. The putrid smell was beginning to grow stronger with the heat from my body, as I realised the floral pattern on my shirt was not exactly as I had bought it.

We had travelled about a mile when tragedy struck – I ran out of petrol! Cursing myself for a fool for forgetting to buy some the day before, I considered my serious predicament. Fortunately, there was a phone box just down the road and I rang the camp. The guardhouse answered and I was put through to 'The Line' where I worked. They duly replied and, praying fervently, I breathlessly asked to be put through to our radio office, my actual place of work. The Gods were with me as Dave Wood answered. He was a dependable married man of some RAF experience, there where he should be, present and on time, exactly where and when I wasn't. I quickly outlined my plight to him, begging him to come and pick us up. Though incredulous, he agreed, bless him. Spanner and I pushed The Pig onto the forecourt of a nearby garage – closed, needless to say – that was several hundred yards down the road. I scribbled a note, put it under the windscreen and we started to walk along the A27 to meet Dave, discussing our position and the previous night's action as we walked.

The last thing I remembered was getting into a stupid drinking contest. A 'Yam-Sing' it was called, taking turns to down large strong drinks in one before someone backed down. My opponent was a fat boozer called Ian Lawson, who had done much more time than me – in the Far East as well. I was well out of my depth and should have known it. Spanner filled in with some helpful details, adding observations about my noisy avowed intention to christen the double bed with Jill, who shared the house with two other nurses. I was practically certain by now that this celebratory consummation could and would not have been possible given the circumstantial evidence, including certain smells and my pounding head. With these in mind, I realised with amazing clarity that Jill might have a few items to discuss with me on my return. If I ever got let out, that was...

The saintly Dave arrived, we bundled ourselves in and, wrinkling his nose with barely-concealed distaste, he confirmed that my absence had been noted socially and, much more worryingly, officially. I should have been there at six o'clock, about the time I opened my eyes. Some helpful early birds were already supplying, spreading and embroidering lurid details of the party, gleaned from a few who had apparently been there. Screeching to a halt outside the 'H' block I lived in, Dave strongly advised me to just throw on my uniform and pick up my travel bag and with luck, we might just make it. I will never forget the disbelieving expression on his face as I told him I hadn't even packed yet.

To sarcastic and witty comments, in the communal room I shared with five others, I heaved on my serge blue uniform, with no time for pleasantries such as washing or shaving, and hoping that the foul stench about me would disappear as I changed. With Dave exhorting at the door for me to 'get a 'kin move on' I quickly threw any cleanish clothes I could find into my RAF-supplied holdall. Resembling a tramp in uniform, I was whizzed up to The Line, where the aircraft sat parked on huge concrete 'pans'. To my horror, the one I should have been on had already started running up its huge, deafening engines. With my hangover it felt as though my head would explode.

I gasped my eternal thanks to Dave, promising to buy him a hundred beers at the next opportunity, as he dropped me right next to the nose of the noisy aircraft. Clutching my holdall, I staggered up the steps that doubled as the door of the enormous Hercules and turned immediately right into the massive hold of the plane, our home for the next six hours. As I came into view, a huge cheer went up and whistles greeted me above the thundering of the engines.

But it was definitely not all good news. Warrant Officer McLeod, the silver-haired detachment leader and administration king of our unit, was sitting immediately on the right and I had to pass him to get to a spare seat. I couldn't help noticing his medals on his 'best blue' uniform. He looked immaculate, of course, especially compared to my dishevelled appearance. Our eyes met and, over the din of the aircraft, he pointed at me and menacingly mouthed the words 'I'll – see – you – in – Cyprus – McGregor!'

I plonked myself down to thumbs-up and laughter from the 'singlies' (unmarried airmen) and shaking-of-heads-in-disbelief from the 'M/Fs' (married with families).

For the following three weeks, on the lovely island of Cyprus, I studiously avoided the 'Warrant' wherever and whenever needed. If he came in, I went out. In the open I would slip quietly behind someone else to hide. I need not have worried really.

It's a closely guarded secret: but there are two Air Forces. The first, and best known to most people, is the 'shiny' Air Force. This is where the grass is painted green, the coal black and aspects such as discipline, marching, 'bull' and saluting are accepted as the norm. It took me about nine months to discover the other Air Force, when I was first sent 'Up The Line' to join this mysterious and fascinating place. In this alternative Air Force, the aircraft is king; everything else takes second place to keeping the planes serviceable, thus enabling 'the other lot' (the aircrew) to fulfil their minor role in actually flying the things.

The reason for going on detachment to Cyprus was to enable the aircrew to get in their required flying hours, mostly by night; not easily done on the South Coast of the UK at that time. Such mundane matters as discipline only concerned the Shiny Air Force, not ours. Here in our crew room I would sit and play cards and drink coffee with young men, who, from the look of them, were the last people on earth you would expect to be serving members of Her Majesty's armed forces. With their droopy *Frank Zappa* moustaches, long hair over their ears and collars, seemingly indifferent attitudes to life and bad language to make your hair curl, their apparent lack of discipline stood out a mile.

But after a while you realised this wasn't the case. Commands were given and accepted, casually yet with mutual respect, and always with the same result... the job got done with little fuss. Occasionally 'requests' (not 'orders') were met with seemingly aggressive protests and language to match. Invariably, these were greeted with a laugh, a shrug and an equally colourful reply; but again, the task was always carried out. Good friendships were born in such circumstances – sometimes under extremely arduous conditions of heat or cold – but good teamwork meant that when the job was done properly, we could then go and party – which we did on almost every available occasion.

The camaraderie I indicated earlier, exemplified by Dave and the banter enjoyed in those days, is something I will never forget. During the four and a half years I worked happily under this 'regime', I travelled the world for free, had many wonderful times and made many friends. One mate I still have today, forty years later. We were 'best men' at each other's weddings and have kept in touch over the years, through life's various trials and tribulations. He still comes to stay with my wife and I every year and we laugh endlessly, reminding each other of the numerous scrapes we got into at that time.

There is one more lasting legacy to this day of that story. It is not a nightmare but a regularly repeated dream I have. I am usually abroad somewhere, normally but not always alone. There is a plane to catch very shortly and I am not ready. In my dream, I have not packed to leave and I am not in the right place to do so; first I have to try to get back to the point where I can start to organise myself. Sometimes I nearly make it, but this is rare. I'm usually floundering around with various minor problems to sort out before I can 'get going'. Without a shadow of doubt, the above experience deeply embedded itself in my subconscious, to come back at seemingly regular intervals.

As ever, I survived to tell the tale of this and other incidents along the way, and nothing formal happened to me as a result of being late. I swear I saw the Warrant wink at me as he passed me a few months later.

For the record, several weeks later, safely back in the UK, the forgiving Jill and I managed to christen the big, comfortable bed properly, without hangovers or Her Majesty calling urgently.

And The Pig was rescued by my good mates while I was in Cyprus, bless 'em. It was all part of a very happy and fun-filled time of my life in the late sixties and early seventies in the Royal Air Force.

2.   If You Can't Take a Joke...

The room suddenly went quiet, apart from a little nervous tittering. The nasty-piece-of-work corporal who was taking our entry to explain the administrative side of the Royal Air Force stopped talking and silently stalked his quarry – a skinny, pimply youth sitting by the window, who had committed the dangerous mistake of gazing out of it. Passing by were a squad of lads in PE gear, doubling along briskly as part of their hour's gym training.

'Now then,' he sneered viciously in the poor lad's ear 'Do you like watching men in shorts, then?' (terrified shake of head). 'Because if you do like watching men in shorts (steadily rising crescendo) I can fix it so that you can watch men in shorts (now shouting) *ALL FUGGIN' DAY! DO YOU UNDERSTAND?*'(the last bit screamed, with dementia). The unfortunate recipient of his bile was made to do ten press-ups on the spot and, from then on, we all hung on the corporal's every boring word. This was administrative basic training at its most brutal and you needed 100% concentration at all times. It was all very exhausting.

When we first arrived at basic training camp at RAF Swinderby in Lincolnshire, transported in the RAF coaches that picked us up from the railway station, we were herded into a big, empty aircraft hangar. There were approximately 120 of us, still dressed in civvies, in our intake that day, Monday 30th January 1967. Funny how I remember the date so clearly! We were lined up along the hangar wall and arranged together in small groups according to the first letter of our surnames. Two mean-looking corporals passed along each group, asking the second and sometimes third letters of our surnames, to form us eventually into a long line in strict alphabetical sequence. I was in 'M' group and when the very nervous lad next to me was asked the next two letters of his surname he mumbled 'um... J.H'. The corporal looked incredulously at the trembling specimen.

'What the fuggin 'ell's your name then?' he demanded.

'John Henry,' came the reply, to gales of nervous laughter.

Now in our new strictly alphabetical line up, with John Henry now safely under P for Preston, we were marched away, if you can call it that, with much apprehension and curiosity; to where, we knew not. I had done four years in the Air Training Corps, the pre-service branch of the RAF, and had a good idea where we were headed. I was right. We were brought to a shambling halt and waited alongside a building, the queue snaking round the corner, with rumour rife of what was about to happen to us. This was to be my first taste of queuing and waiting, which was something I would get used to. It was to occupy a great deal of my time during the next five years. You were always waiting for something: food, pay, aircraft landing, issues of almost everything. But in these early days it was uniform measurements, health checks (drop your trousers, cough...), dentists, drills (marching, not dental) and numerous injections. I was totally cleared of any slight fears of these after sometimes two or three per day for the first week – "just a small prick..." went the joke.

In this particular case, word was quickly passed down the line that we were steadily approaching the camp barber, although 'butcher' would have been more appropriate. There were two barbers at work in their 'salon', with the radio on loud, and it was popularly touted that each man could carry out three military-style haircuts per record played. My father was an ex-services disciplinarian where hair was concerned; I didn't know until I was sixteen that there was any other type of haircut than 'short back and sides'. For the last year before joining up, I had been a scooter-riding 'Mod' and part of our 'uniform' was short hair anyway, so mercifully I had little trouble. But the biggest laugh was to see the faces of the idiots who actually came to join up with long hair; it seemed the barbers reserved the shortest, most vicious cuts for such dipsticks. Their faces were a study as they tried to laugh off being reduced to the appearance of convicts in a matter of seconds.

It was fuggin' freezing during February 1967 in cold, flat, windswept Lincolnshire. In the very basic wooden Nissen huts where we were living during our eight weeks basic training, there were central stoves which we huddled round to keep warm before going to bed, which was usually early by 10.30 pm at the very latest.

This is because were always shattered and needed to be up early to be able to cope with the very physical and mental days, which began at five-thirty. At this ungodly hour you would rise and head for the communal bathrooms to wash, shave and perhaps briefly bath or shower.

Very quickly and brutally any inhibitions one may have previously harboured about taking one's clothes off in public were smashed. Quite simply, there was nowhere to hide in a long narrow room, beds either side, full of seventeen other men, all there for the same purpose. No matter how big, small, fat, thin, long, tall or short you were in any department, there was always someone bigger, smaller, fatter, thinner, longer, taller or shorter than you in every way. In any case, dimensions were roundly discussed and extremes pointed out. Mercifully, I did not qualify for too much of such verbal examination, being 'one of the lads' in every way, which suited me.

Sex was a favourite subject, of course, and I seem to remember that circumcision was a regular topic: foreskin, or the lack of it, the pros and cons, etc, were discussed at length (pardon the expression). As in any walk of life, there were the braggers, the exhibitionists, those who took delight in exhibiting their credentials at every possible opportunity, captured wonderfully by the film *The Virgin Soldiers,* as in.

Bragger, staring at willy in hand: 'I'm sure this blue vein is getting bigger, do you think I should show it to the MO (Medical Officer)?'

Witty riposte: 'Well, why miss him out, you've shown to everyone else on the camp!'

Clothing quickly became a big issue, in that ALL civilian clothing you wore to travel on joining up, or that you may have brought with you, despite specific instructions not to, was ceremoniously inspected, parcelled up and then sent back to your home by post, leaving you only with issued uniform and shoes to wear. Putting on one's uniform was still a novelty at this stage; it was amazing how coarse it felt to your young skin. We laughed at each other as we saw those recent 'civvies', now abruptly transformed for the first time into real servicemen. There was a lot to learn about our uniforms, including how to 'bull' our boots and shoes into a parade-acceptable shine, which took many hours of evening elbow-grease.

Then there was the regulation traditional bed-pack to learn about. This involved stripping the bed so that the only item covering the mattress was the thin, striped bed cover, and then learning how to build this strange object. Basically the idea was to produce a final, regulation-sized 'sandwich', where one blanket, folded lengthwise, was wrapped around three others in a differently folded format, between which were sandwiched the two sheets, all folded carefully to the same size. To begin with, this was extremely tedious to master, involving many expletives and angry demolitions (about five hundred I would estimate before you started to get the hang of it) but eventually the task could be achieved in about ten painful minutes.

Then between six and six-thirty it was breakfast. I really can't remember anything notable about this meal, as I have always been a dustbin where food is concerned – still am, come to think of it. It was just essential fuel for the coming day's exertions: greasy eggs, bacon, sausages, beans, tinned tomatoes, toast, tea and/or coffee. It didn't do to have a weak stomach and I didn't, due to coming from a big family where you had to fight your corner to get your share. So where plenty was available suited me well. 'Just eat and don't worry about it,' was my motto. Incidentally, both tea and coffee tasted the same, although rumours abounded that they were laced with 'bromide' to stop you getting *those* feelings – although we didn't have the time or the inclination (one way of putting it) for anything like that, anyway.

After breakfast was a worrying time when you had to make sure you were dressed and shined, bed-pack rearranged, with nerves beginning to jangle as the dreaded 7 am approached. This hour was 'inspection time' – a time to be either highly anxious or reasonably cool, depending on who was doing the inspecting. Initially we had the short, stocky Corporal Brown, he of the slashed peak and mean, moody appearance. Well, we thought *he* was mean and moody, but little did we know that he was a mere pussycat compared to what was to come. We had Brown for the first introductory week. Everyone thought the initial training, and he himself, were very hard as he shouted, cursed, effed and blinded at us as we tried to learn to march in lines, turn right or left or stop together at the same time.

Just as we thought we were making progress and getting it, the world took an amazing leap into the unknown. On the Monday morning of the second week, with the one week induction over, the full seven weeks basic training began – and Potting arrived!

Corporal Potting was about 6ft 2 ins tall, thin like a ramrod and absolutely immaculately dressed, almost making Brown look scruffy by comparison, which he wasn't. But the most terrifying aspects of Potting's armoury were his voice and body language. He didn't speak, he howled in an almost demented, controlled shriek as he literally screamed out his orders, as though permanently struggling to contain his rage. This very discordant, maniacal note struck terror into the young hearts of we new recruits. Most of us visibly shook under his verbal onslaught; I certainly did. He didn't appear to breathe deeply but his neck would seem to protrude about a foot from his shoulders as he roared at us, eyes bulging, blood vessels pumping.

He was a fearful sight and it was a terrifying thing for a seemingly-innocent young man to have a fully-grown apparent lunatic, dressed in immaculately superior uniform, screaming into your face from about two inches away, with accompanying spit and vile temper, because you had displeased him in some way that you couldn't comprehend. You vowed there and then to never, ever repeat such a mistake; and you didn't. Punishments for such misdemeanours were doubling around the parade square with your rifle held above your head or completing umpteen press-ups in full uniform until Potting ordered you to stop.

Like most drill NCOs (Non-Commissioned Officers) Potting had that peculiar vision that could apparently see things that displeased him at an angle of ninety degrees to looking straight forward. While wildly staring ahead and apparently concentrating straight in front, he would shoot his right or left arm at right angles, pointing accusingly at some terrified blue-uniformed airman and scream obscenities accordingly at whatever displeased him. You just could not relax, it was as if he saw everything and missed nothing. You never heard or saw Potting coming; one minute he wasn't there, the next second he was, his face purple, straining as if he were plugged into the mains. He shouted, screamed, swore and threatened us, until at last we began to get it; that magical obedience that all trained servicemen possess, so that when someone shouts 'duck!' you instinctively do it, perhaps at some later time saving your life in the process. Normal people ask 'why?' when ordered to duck – and get their heads blown off!

As the majority started to get it, the slower ones developed more and more paranoia as they became steadily more isolated and noticeable to Potting, who delighted in singling them out for specific individual abuse, where one's parents, their marital status and their offspring's legal status were frequently brought into question.

But licked into shape, we were by his constant bullying and threats. Over the seven weeks, without noticing it yourself, you became an efficient, fully-fit member of Her Majesty's Armed Forces. You could march, turn, salute, present and shoulder arms, and be on parade by seven each morning with all your issue laid out for inspection inside your billet by your bed. You were not an individual now, you were a number, rank and name – A4287990 AC McGregor in my case.

3.   It Ain't Half Cold, Mum!

'Send reinforcements, we're going to advance!' By the time the message had been passed down the line through three hundred raw young army recruits, it was reported as 'Send three and fourpence, we're going to a dance! So runs the famous old forces-training joke and in February 1968, aboard a very noisy Hercules aircraft somewhere over the Alps, I had a similar experience of mixed-up messages being passed up the line. We were returning to our base in the southern UK from three weeks in the desert in Libya, dressed accordingly in KD – Khaki Drill uniform, as made popular in the tv series *It Ain't Half Hot, Mum*. Cramped in the noisy aircraft, the rumours began to circulate, originating from the aircrew on the flight deck.

Passing on and embroidering these rumours served a dual purpose; it helped to pass a very uncomfortable, boring few hours in the air and it also helped to wind up the 'scalies' (married men), who had promised their wives and their families they would be home safely on a certain date. Any variation in such arrangements caused them concern and so the twisted forces sense of humour ensured that we 'singlies' extracted the maximum worry possible from the situation. At one time we were mischievously telling them we had to return to Libya, a horrible prospect; untrue, but amusing to see the look on their faces.

As it happened though, the rumours of closure of our home base due to inclement weather conditions that were reaching us were actually true, even though we wildly exaggerated them. Our southern base was usually climate-friendly, so the story seemed strange; but as the time aboard moved on, it seemed certain that we would be diverted. But where to? The southern half of England seemed to be affected by heavy falls of snow, so it seemed no RAF station of any size was exempt from suggestion; even Scotland was mentioned, scaly faces whitening by the minute. You would think servicemen and their wives and families would be accustomed to such uncertainties – apparently not!

After a great deal of speculation, it was confirmed that Abingdon, near Oxford was our destination, which although under three feet of snow itself, had managed to clear enough runway for us to land, which we did in mid-afternoon. The bitter cold hit us as soon as we were out of our aircraft, we must have looked a comical sight dressed in only our thin khaki uniforms; over half of us were only dressed in shorts and short-sleeved shirts. We hurried across the pan, the concrete base the planes are parked on, without one coat of any sort between the sixty or so of us. You don't need coats in the desert!

Back inside, in the warm, we sipped tea and were given two options. The first option was that we could be housed temporarily for the night in Abingdon and, hopefully, driven back to Thorney Island by RAF transport the next day. Many roads had been cut off due to the weather and little spare functional transport was available until at least the next day, so there were no guarantees that this would happen anyway. The second option was to travel back straight away by rail, which was said to still be operating, although on a restricted basis. To my surprise, almost everyone plumped for the second option. I would have been happy to stay put and take pot luck but Abingdon RAF Station was not liked by some and, of course, all the worried scalies wanted to get home. Wouldn't be anything to do with sex, would it? There had been none of that for anyone in Libya...

There was one proviso with this latter option, however, namely that a special railway warrant was needed to authorise the journey. We were promised it was on the way, so back out into the cold we went, and were transported in very uncomfortable three-tonners (open heavy trucks) to Abingdon railway station. This proved to be a tiny, one-platform affair, which, when full of sixty-odd freezing, swearing, shivering, bad-tempered airmen, in thin khaki clothing, rapidly achieved the element of farce. Speculation quickly ran round the bitterly cold platform that the train was due in twenty minutes. There wasn't another for an hour after that, so where was the fuggin' rail warrant?

One or two in vague command, by dint of higher rank, though not wishing to enforce it, murmured that we should all wait for the warrant until it came, irrespective of whether the right train had come. But this was a working aircraft unit, where such matters as discipline, rigid orders, saluting and other such bullshitty methods used elsewhere in the RAF and the other services did not apply normally to us – and definitely did not apply that day, not on Ice Station Abingdon.

Yes, the train came, and no, no warrant had arrived. It only took one to break ranks, not that there were any 'ranks', just a bunch of khaki-clad young men whose testicles were well and truly freezing, and we all ran like hell, cramming ourselves into the tiny, three-carriage local train until there was no room anywhere. The few bemused civilian travellers on the train must have been astounded by what hit them; the language was appalling as we all vainly fought for a seat.

The train slowly pulled out and we were on our way.

Two changes of trains were necessary en route, at Reading and at Portsmouth. The best laugh was when a ticket inspector got on, which happened twice. Of course, everyone told him the warrant holder was further down the train. By the time the poor sap had worked his way through the packed carriageways, it was time to change trains and wait like brass monkeys for the next one. With the temperature dropping as evening approached, we had to hop, skip and dance (and curse, of course) around the platform to keep warm before the next train came. We got some very strange looks from the unfortunate commuters.

Soon darkness came and it began to snow again. The burning question, about which there was much debate, was this – assuming we reached our final rail destination in the village near the camp, we would then be about a mile and a half from home. The one clapped-out bus service from the village to the camp was a law unto itself and stopped running the minute anything untoward ensued, like bad weather. The twisty and very treacherous road on the camp (which was actually on an island just off the South Coast) was also notoriously dangerous, so we were reasonably certain that the bus would not be running; and we were right. Now a new element arose; could those who had friends or relatives manage to contact them, in order that they could riskily come out to meet and rescue some of the lucky ones? And would those fortunate people:

a) be prepared to give lifts to some of those less fortunate? and

b) would said friends and relatives then be prepared to return and collect any others?

All sorts of relationships began to form, founder, then reform, as loyalties were tested and old dues called in. You soon found out who your real friends were. By the time we finally arrived in the village late in the evening and abandoned the protection of the train, it was snowing hard onto freezing ice. There were three cars waiting in the tiny car park, with windscreen wipers going frantically and a dozen or so lucky souls crammed in. We watched them enviously as they disappeared down the slippery road into the darkness. We slithered and skidded our way through the deserted village, eerie now in the fresh snow, soon soaked to the skin, our thin khaki shirts, shorts, socks and shoes, designed for heat and sun, offering little protection against the elements. I have never been more grateful for my blue beret, pulled right down over my ears; I always knew it would come in handy one day!

In the event, no-one walked the whole way back. After a while, we promised each other that if we got back ok then, somehow, by hook or by crook, we would return for the others. And, as well trained serviceman and mates – we did.

With us all being so young and fit, nobody caught pneumonia or suffered badly as a result but it was an experience I will never forget. I have never looked forward to my bed as much as I did that night, after a hot shower had restored the circulation. The following day we could see the funny side and laughed about it, although there wasn't too much of that about at the time!

The RAF motto is *Per Ardua ad Astra* – which means 'through toil to the skies' – but it doesn't mean freezing your Jacobs' off for hours on a snowy station platform, dressed as if you were helping Monty fight Rommel in the desert, as had happened twenty-five years previously. The things I did for my Queen and Country!

4.　Sergeant Pepper

'*It was twenty years ago today, Sgt Pepper taught the band to play....*'
So runs the opening line of one of the greatest albums in rock
history. It is actually over forty years ago since *The Beatles* released
the *Sergeant Pepper* LP, in the summer of 1967; the year that is
remembered as the 'Flower Power' era of peace, love, hippies, and
pop festivals.

In April 1967 I was not into flowers or long hair; far from it. I was
embarking on a four-month trade training course in basic aircraft
radio mechanics. That was the year the pirate radio stations were
finishing and Radio One was starting up, Tony Blackburn, *et al*. In
stark contrast to all this peace and love around, the only music in
our eighteen-man room was supplied by one of our number who
possessed a Dansette record player, with – guess how many
records? Two, actually, yes just two LPs between us, for four
months. One was a live recording of the Beach Boys in concert,
which started by an American voice introducing the group as 'And
now, from Pasadena California, we present, the fabulous... Beach
Boys!'

'*If everybody had an ocean, across the USA...*' went the opening
line of 'Surfin' USA'. I knew every line of every song, even what they
said between numbers. The other LP was, of course, the great
'Sergeant Pepper', arguably the greatest Beatles album of the lot,
and I can recite it all off by heart. I should be able to, I heard it
enough. The two were played incessantly, over and over again, but
strangely enough I never tired of them!

From April to July of that year, apart from the music there wasn't
much of the above peace and love type of frivolity, in fact it was a
very difficult period of my life. There were several reasons for this:
the first and most important was the fact that I was embarking on
the second and most mentally challenging period of training in my
new-found military career. I was required to complete and pass a
four-month trade training course in my chosen field, which was

aircraft radio systems, or to give it its full exotic name, Electronic Mechanic, Air Communications.

What I had not realised, but should have by this time, was that I am not really cut out for any type of scientific work. I should have realised it from school where I struggled badly with physics and chemistry, but the penny had not dropped by then. Of the eighteen of us on the course, at least six were already qualified lads from civvy street, who had done apprenticeships and attended college in electronic-type industries, but they were finding work hard to come by so had decided to join up. Needless to say, after two to three years studying such stuff already, they found it easy. I didn't.

Unfortunately coupled with this, back at home my lovely Mum was going through a difficult period of her life with her nerves. For some years, after a very busy time raising four demanding children as we moved around the country, the pace of life had begun to slacken and Mum began to have doubts about herself. Her self-confidence suffered, and she began to take to her bed more and more often to 'rest'.

Matters had lately come to a head as I started the course, so much so that when I went home for the first free weekend, about two weeks into the course, I found she had been admitted to the local mental hospital for such complaints. This was a place we had all joked about at school as we grew up, the city 'nut-house' where all the seriously barmy people went. To go and visit my own mother in such a place, in a big ward with some fellow inmates who seemed to fit the expected bill was a harrowing experience for me.

My Mum had always been there for me as I grew up, I loved her very much and took her for granted, as kids do. To see that she had deteriorated so considerably and quickly was very upsetting. To make matters worse, when visiting time was over, Mum threw her arms round my neck in a vice-like grip, imploring me not to go, as I was "*the only one who understands*". I took this very seriously and returned to camp a worried young man. Much later, I found this was a favourite ploy of Mum's, she used with us all, but at the time I felt a tremendous personal pressure on my young shoulders.

Back at camp, the training course ritual meant that you were in a classroom from eight am to five pm Monday to Thursday, and eight am until lunchtime Friday. Then, first thing after lunch, was a heavy exam, based on what you had learned that week. The pass mark was sixty per cent and if you didn't pass, you were called back in immediately and made to do a re-sit. If you didn't pass that, you were out, with shame and disgrace heaped upon you. From memory, we lost several lads early on, but somehow, and not easily, I just scraped through, week by week, to stay with it.

But there were pranksters, wind-up merchants and piss-takers and one of my abiding memories is coming back after the evening meal and lying on my bed, stiff and rigid as a board, quivering with pent-up anger ready to explode if anyone 'tried it on' with me. I can only actually remember one real fight and that was with a mate, Dave from London, a wise guy who was always larking around. As I recall, it was a short-lived affair, rolling around on the floor locked together for a few minutes before it somehow fizzled out. I think it was mostly pent-up frustration about my mother's situation that made me so tense inside, although I also felt the weekly exam pressure very keenly.

There was some light relief. Dave had a Bedford Dormobile van, with bench seats, which could hold seven easily. We had heard about a Cider House out in the sticks and one weekday evening we set out to find it. Dave had managed the impossible in befriending a pretty WAAF, a remarkable feat considering the female of the species was heavily outnumbered on our station – by about a hundred to one, I should estimate. He succeeded largely because he had transport and, at the last minute that evening, his girl came too. She was also, ominously, accompanied by her fat, spotty, unattractive pal. On the way there, sober, we lads dug each other in the ribs, indicating one of us would get off with the mate before the evening was out. Hmm...

We found the cider house and discovered there were three grades of cider: it cost one shilling and threepence for a pint of the best stuff, ninepence for the averagely mind-blowing cider and sixpence for the rotgut, blow-your-head-off, rocket fuel with bits of apples floating in it – scrumpy, in other words. If you have ever been in the services, you know exactly what's coming – the sixpenny pint – which was so strong it flew so straight to your head and you could feel yourself going during the first one. Some were sensible and left it like that, just having one, but a few of us – me included – tried to drink a second half pint. Big mistake!

I very, very dimly remember rolling around on the floor at the back of the Dormobile, trying very ineffectively to do something sexually naughty to the attractively-challenged WAAF. Half-way down my first pint, Dave had whispered to me that Quasimodo had confided to her friend that she fancied me and, all of a sudden, through the golden light of fermented apple-juice, she didn't look too bad. By the time I had finished the pint she looked ravishing and after the extra half, well... she was inebriated too and fitted the bill!

Needless to say, apart from some seriously ineffective groping and hoping, we slid all over the place as Dave's alcohol-assisted driving round the bends right out in the country hurled us around. We had to stop when Quaz was sick everywhere. That literally put a damper on everything, so action of any sort stopped there and then! I had to endure some serious extraction of the uric acid for the next few days, as those who hadn't made the trip were colourfully regaled regarding the intimate details of my amorous advances, some of which were new even to me, although I had apparently been involved.

I did take out one attractive young lady of the district during that period and I remember we went to the pictures in Wolverhampton, to see *Privilege,* with Jean Shrimpton and Paul Jones, previously of Manfred Mann fame. We caught the bus to take her home and found ourselves alone on the top deck. We were kissing and cuddling, quite strongly, and I thought all was going well, so I put my hand gently firstly on her knee, no resistance, and thus encouraged, successfully slipped it round to the inside of her lower thigh.

All seemed well; I was ambitiously climbing higher, with no stoppages, and the summit was in sight when she lifted up her non-groped leg and crossed it firmly over and on top of my hand, effectively trapping it in an almost vice-like grip. I was perfectly stymied and, short of standing up, placing my foot on her thigh and pulling hard, there was nothing I could do, so we passed a long bus journey in this manner until it was her stop. It took me ages to get the circulation back in my hand. I learnt a lot that day. I promised to phone her the next day, but didn't, as I felt by this time I was out of my depth in seduction techniques. I spent hours trying to work out what I should do the next time in similar circumstances. I'm still no wiser, by the way. Luckily, it never happened again – any ideas lads?

Back to the course, I struggled through somehow; some weeks were agonisingly difficult but I survived. The final exam lasted three hours and covered everything we had learned on the course, but somehow I passed and at last the ordeal was over.

Mum was a bit better. She had come home after a few weeks in that horrible place but she was far from the happy, funny Mum I had grown up with. My Dad was very strong-willed, no shades of grey when it came to mental matters, and he just didn't get it. Not that I did, really, but I always tried to be sympathetic.

When I was posted to the South Coast, further from home than I had ever lived, I am ashamed to say I considered cutting all ties with home. I just couldn't take it when Mum piled on the pressure, telling me that nobody else understood, only me. I couldn't tell anyone else, although we have always been a close family. I felt I had a huge secret that I couldn't share with anyone. The Sergeant Pepper song *'She's leaving home'* was a bit poignant at that time for me, the lyrics said it all. The Mum's words *why would she treat us so thoughtlessly – how could she do this to me?* perfectly summed up how I thought Mum would see it if I really left home – for good.

But that posting actually freed me, in a way. At last I had finished training, the pressure was off and the big, wide world beckoned. And it was the summer of love! I travelled down south to our new posting with another bloke from our course, Paul Aylott, who I didn't like much, and that's documented elsewhere. We travelled down from the Midlands to the South Coast together in his car and, nearing our destination, stopped for lunch at a fairly new pub called 'The Winston Churchill' on Portsdown Hill, a famous local beauty spot which, looking south over the coastline, gives a wonderful panoramic view of Portsmouth (actually Portsea Island, if you don't know), Hayling Island – which would prove to be my regular fertile stamping ground and – last but definitely not least – Thorney Island, the picturesque Royal Air Force station which was to become my home for the next four and a half years.

As I stood and gazed out from the pub garden on that sunny July day in that suddenly-exciting year of 1967, I can still recall the buzz, the anticipation, the thrill of at last really getting away from home, spreading my wings and beginning to fly (see how the Air Force had really got to me?). I had no idea at all of what was in store for me at that stage, and I didn't care much either. Strangely enough, I felt I was in charge of my own destiny for once, even though I was a serviceman in Her Majesty's Armed Forces.

Little did I know what a roller-coaster ride the next four and a half years were to be, a melange of fun, women, excitement, booze, music, RAF life, aircraft, highs and lows, cars and characters, although definitely not in that, or any other order; just really a transition from boy to man, I suppose. I didn't cut my ties with home, realistically I couldn't anyway; my family was the rock I built my life on. I just left it a while before I went home for a weekend; by then I was having a ball and wanted to go home and share it all. Things seemed better when I did go, although Mum was still having problems. But I suppose I dealt with these better as I was much happier and not under the constant pressures of trade training and those bloody exams every week.

So I said good-bye to *Sergeant Pepper* and the Beach Boys and all that intensive training. I was now allowed out, blinking into the summer sunshine, to get on with the next stage of my life. Although from the Beatles' *Abbey Road* album in 1969, *Here comes the Sun* expresses my mood that day on Portsdown Hill in 1967.

I've heard the sixties described as the decade when the world went from black and white to colour. Well, this perfectly describes my leaving home in the industrial Midlands and moving to the sunny South Coast. I was excited and ready for some fun!

5.   The Hercules

From my vantage point in the air, I looked down at the advancing C130 Lockheed Hercules as it approached the aircraft carrier. Surely, I thought, that huge transport aircraft is not going to attempt to land on the carrier! But yes, the 'Herc' lined up and prepared to land and I held my heart in my mouth. The pilot put the plane down immediately at the beginning of the (very) short runway, she bounced once gently before the colossal thrust of full reverse was immediately applied, and the Herc safely screeched to a stop with full brakes on, with what seemed only a little runway to spare – phew!

'And if you think that was scary, watch this,' said the corporal running the film we were watching. To our amazement, from the same angle, presumably shot from a helicopter hovering near the carrier, the Herc re-appeared at the edge of the runway, with all four engines screaming away but not moving, presumably with brakes full on. Suddenly the back dropped, the nose lifted a little as the plane surged forward, slowly at first, then with increasing pace hurtled along the short runway towards the edge.

'No chance,' I thought. 'She'll just go straight over into the sea'. But I was wrong and although she seemed to dip a little as she swept over the edge of the carrier, she picked up like a giant silver bird and steadily gained height. All I can say is that I'm glad I wasn't aboard at the time...

During a specialised Hercules course at RAF Lyneham I was watching a training film on the Hercules supplied by the makers Lockheed, designed to tell us more about the amazing aircraft we would be working on. The film demonstrated the versatility of the aircraft as Lockheed put it through its paces back in America. Some of it I already knew; I had seen for myself the ability of the Hercules to taxi backwards when full reverse thrust was applied, a noisy but effective manoeuvre.

The Hercules was not the biggest workhorse in the RAF at the time, there were gigantic aircraft like Galaxies at RAF Fairford, where you could hold a dance in the hold with a stage at one end, although these were huge, lumbering affairs. But for middle-sized loads like a small truck, 300 paratroopers, God knows how many boxes of whatever supplies, the Herc had no equal for fast, safe delivery around the world, coupled with an enormous fuel capacity to fly over oceans. Personally I flew over a few as a passenger, although I have to say they were very uncomfortable, especially when enduring a flight in excess of thirteen hours to cross the Atlantic – but their safety record is first-class.

For groundcrew they were good planes to work on – requiring maintenance, yes, but not unpleasant or difficult to work on, although I was a radio mechanic, so relatively simple black box changing was my forte. To do my job meant taking away the steps leading from the main hold up to the Flight deck, you were roundly cursed by the other trades as they struggled to get up and down without the ladder. The ladder protected a tunnel, accessible on your hands and knees, where on either side were situated the black boxes that made up the radio and radar systems. Most of the systems were comprised of either three, four or five black metal boxes, marked A, B, C, etc, and any malfunction was almost always to be found within one of the boxes. We kept spare boxes in our stores, so when a 'snag' was reported by the aircrew, it usually pointed to one or other of the boxes. Simple elimination of these in turn usually cured the fault and the aircraft was made serviceable again in a very short time. That was 'first-line servicing', which I did happily for about four years on the Hercs. Very simple but very effective in keeping the aircraft flying as easily and quickly as possible.

I was a 'fairy' – along with radar, navigation instruments and electricians, known as *fairies* by our more robust colleagues who worked in the manly trades of airframes and engines. They were known as *heavies* for obvious reasons. Obviously engines did what it said on the tin, so if you added their forte to our 'fairy' skills, if you then take that from the complete aircraft technical puzzle – everything (and I mean everything) left over was the province of airframes, known colloquially as 'riggers', who were the lowest of the low, trades-wise. Sorry, my rigger friends, make that the most hard-working, put-upon of all the six trades. Who else would be emptying aircraft loos, cleaning up everything – and I mean *everything* – which brings me to one of those 'unbelievable but true' stories that exist only in the forces. It runs like this...

There is, or was, a division of the RAF called The Queen's Flight, which existed to fly members of The Royal Family, prominent politicians or such equivalent luminaries around the world. It sounded glamorous but in truth The Queen's Flight was far from that. The groundcrew were a hard-bitten, put-upon outfit who had to turn out almost anytime at a moment's notice at the whim of those VIPs and Royals who needed to go somewhere fast. So the story ran that on one particular flight a very prominent member of The Royal Family, who shall remain nameless, was forced to use the loo on board the plane, dropping a 'full-load', so to speak, during the journey. As the personage involved had the exclusive use of that loo, what they 'left behind' was undoubtedly theirs ... so the animals who serviced the plane duly rescued the said item, varnished it and put it in a glass case, like a prized salmon, for display in the crewroom, where it proudly displayed a plaque which read 'XXXXXX's turd. I heard this from a couple of different sources during my time, so it must be true![2]

Yes, riggers got all the shitty jobs, literally as well as theoretically. But for all that they remained a cheerful bunch, hardy and thorough, good lads to have on your side, and they took a bit of stick. Their favourite weapon – sorry, tool – was a huge solid screwdriver, which could be used in a myriad of ways, to lever, prise or batter troublesome items encountered in the course of their work. The official name for this essential item was a GS13479 or some such number (everything in the forces has some such number or letters to identify it) but it was simply known colloquially as a 'GS'. Therefore the riggers had their own verb in their specialised operations, that we others didn't possess – 'to GS it' – meaning to use the screwdriver with whatever force and in whatever fashion was necessary to get the job done. After I had left

---

[2] *A History of the King's Flight and The Queen's Flight* was published by Woodfield in 2003 but makes no mention of this particular incident! Ed.

the RAF, from time to time in my life when a little brute force was needed to accomplish something, I would think to myself, 'I know... I'll GS it!'

After I had been 'up the line' some months, the slightly quirky duty of 'earlies' came up. This shift was part of the day shift, it is an earlier version of normal days. To a lazy little toad like me, it was bad enough having to get up to start work at seven o'clock and work until four thirty, so when there was a chance of doing the early shift, I thought 'that's for me', for several reasons. On earlies, you went in at five am (the downside) but when the dayshift came in at seven, you cleared off for breakfast. Although officially this was only for one hour, you could spin if out until at least eight-thirty to nine, sometimes even later, as the main work was always being done, so nobody missed you. But the biggest bonus of all was that you finished for good at twelve-thirty. A quick kip after lunch to compensate for getting up at five and the rest of the day was yours.

Of course, after a while, in typical forces fashion, I even managed to abuse that position by not going in early at all, hoping that, in the darkness, I wouldn't be missed, then coming in, supposedly back from breakfast, around nine. But before long, an eagled-eyed young sergeant spotted that one and checked me out one morning to find me still in bed at 7.30. I was taken off earlies for a week as a punishment but there was no one else who wanted to do it, so I got the job back – with a warning.

Earlies were mainly for the heavies, when certain important things had to be done by the poor old riggers only. We fairies had little to do but there was one balls-aching task that we were ripe for – de-icing. On some bitterly cold mornings, if the official control tower temperature thermometer said so, the planes flying first thing had to be de-iced. What a pain it was – and we fairies were always caught for it, the heavies suddenly conveniently engrossing themselves in their work. For once, their trade came up trumps and we were lumbered. The de-icing tanker was sent for, which had been plugged into the mains all night, to keep the necessary water and glycol mixture correct. The de-icing wagon, looking like a normal petrol tanker but with a vertical wooden turret sticking up above it, would park near the leading edge of the Herc's wings and a poor sap like me, unused to heavy physical work, would climb up the turret.

Standing inside the top bit, in the waist-high compartment, you would grasp a long metal tube with a firing nozzle on one end and the other attached to a hose pipe that ran down into the tank. By pressing a lever on the tube, a fine spray was emitted though the nozzle and directed onto the leading edge of the wing. The problem was always that the sticky, smelly mixture would, by dint of gravity and the 'angle of dangle' necessary to hold and aim the thing, run in a trickle down the aimer's arms, inside his clothing and find its way around the body. Nice, especially first thing on an icy morning! We all dreaded it when the early shift controller suspected the outdoor temperature and rang the tower. Cue for much bad language if it triggered de-icing! But apart from that, and having to get up at 4.45 am, in my book the pros outweighed the cons, so I always opted for the early shift.

In my humble opinion, as a radio mechanic who did black box changing and basic aircraft handling, I loved the Hercules. Anyone who has served in the RAF at the sharp end will point out that I never knew anything else, which is true, but I travelled many miles in these aircraft and grew to appreciate their blunt tactical use in a modern air force – the ability to carry loads and people from A to B, quickly and safely. I was sad to see that one of our old Hercules aircraft – XV179 – was shot down in Iraq in 2005. Their safety record is impeccable.

No wonder many Hercules are still flying today, after thousands of hours. It means those fabulous aircraft are still fully serviceable forty-odd years on. Are there still cars like that about? Not many, it would seem, but the brave Herc carries on – what an aircraft!

6.   ...You Shouldn't Have Joined

Halfway through basic induction, after four weeks a strange turn of events occurred. With almost no notice, one evening we were told to pack our RAF holdalls with all our equipment and be ready first thing in the morning to travel – but where were we going? I was to learn, along with everyone else, that the rumour machine was alive and well in my service days. Some people just delighted in starting dubious stories of what was going to happen shortly, in the hope of winding the more gullible up to believe them, and it often worked. 'ABC' had started – forces-speak for 'All Bin Changed'(sic). Rumours were rife that war had broken out and we were being sent heaven-knows-where. It was all quite possible, given that we had very little outside knowledge of what was happening, there being no TVs or radios allowed in basic training.

Early next morning we were herded into three-ton trucks, *à la* World War Two and driven off to... Sherwood Forest! We were to camp for seven days in the Forest, and yes, we had snow, because it was mid-February! Coming from nearby Nottingham, as I did, I knew Sherwood Forest reasonably well; it is about 20 miles north of Nottingham. Very nice to visit on a warm summer's afternoon with a picnic and see *The Major Oak*, a huge old oak tree alleged to have been Robin Hood's lair in The Middle Ages, but hardly where you would wish to spend a week camping in February. It was fuggin' freezing, as we all told each other – repeatedly!

When we arrived we had to build our camp, each of us deployed in different sections. I was assigned to help erect the cookhouse, a large marquee which took us a couple of hours to build. When we stopped for a meal, one keen observer remarked that the toilets were 'not for the faint-hearted'. When pressed on this point, he elaborated that there was no privacy; it was 'open house'. Horrified, yet drawn like a moth to a flame, I went to the toilet tent and peeped in.

My worst fears were confirmed, for inside there was an open line of temporary sit-down affairs under which various holes had apparently been dug. Loo paper was collected on the way in. I just could not believe that this very private exercise (not a spectator sport as far as I was concerned) was to be conducted in public and privately vowed that I would not be taking part, under any circumstances. I acquired a quantity of my own loo paper and made my own arrangements, deep in the forest, during the next week. At my own convenience, you might say. Others did not seem to share my concerns however, breezily coming and going with little apparent problem, with hearty humour and few inhibitions it seemed. Not for me, Tommy!

Apart from freezing our nuggets off for a week, on several route marches, treks and a lot of swearing during the week, we returned happily back to camp, albeit the real sort of camp, hard-but-luxurious real beds and four walls, even if they were wooden. Neither Potting or Brown had been with us on this 'holiday'. Specialized hardy outward-bound types took care of us with no real problems other than the bitter cold.

On returning we had only three weeks to go before posting to our trade training courses. Naturally apprehensive of Potting, we were pleasantly surprised when, despite our being outside lined up at seven am for inspection on the following Monday morning, Brown ambled up at 7.05 and put us through our paces at a reasonable canter, away from the demented, highly-charged anxiety-ridden regime Potting excelled in. No-one initially dared to ask but later in the day, over a Naafi break[3] someone bravely asked where Corporal Potting was. We were gravely informed that 'Attila the Hun' – our words, not Brown's – was off sick with an ulcer. How

---

[3] Here I should explain that Naafi breaks quickly become an important part of service life. Everything, and I mean everything, comes to a halt from ten to ten-thirty in the mornings and three to three-thirty in the afternoons, when everyone downs tools and drinks tea or coffee. In addition, Wednesday afternoons were regarded as sacrosanct in the forces, designated as sports afternoons when little actual work took place. So the standing forces joke became that the ideal time to attack Britain was any weekday morning between ten and ten thirty, any afternoon between three and three-thirty or any Wednesday afternoon, as the UK was virtually undefended at those times.

sad! We all relaxed visibly for the rest of the week as we continued going through the motions with Brown, silently offering our prayers to the almighty.

Another week went by and we began to visibly relax as we only had one more week before our passing-out parade. Life with Brown in charge was quite acceptable; he growled a lot but nothing more sinister. But at five to seven on the final Monday morning, with the passing-out parade due on the Friday, a terrifying thing happened. We had gone through the normal routine of getting ready to be on parade outside for seven o'clock, breakfasted and with our kit laid out for inspection on our beds, when suddenly a horrifying noise erupted. It sounded almost like an animal squealing in pain and we looked at each other, frozen in terror.

'Fugginell, it's Potting!' someone shouted, and we ran hell-for-leather for the door. To not be in place on parade when Potting arrived was to subject oneself to vile abuse and humiliating public torture, as we had all witnessed and some had suffered. To put it mildly, we were petrified. Fortunately, our room was at the back of the block. The front two rooms took the brunt of his wrath and by the time he rounded the corner we were where we should be, albeit literally quaking in our boots. With a facial shade somewhere between purple and black, the fearsome voice from hell erupted.

'No wonder I've got fuggin' ulcers with you lot!' Potting screamed. 'You fuggin' useless shower of shit are the biggest waste of space I've ever seen in my life!'

I may not have got that observation exactly right, but the first bit was verbatim. I will never forget it or the way it was delivered. The next few days we were on a knife-edge, paranoid whenever Potting was around. But the great day of passing-out came at last and our folks arrived: Mums, Dads, sweethearts, wives, siblings and friends to see us march proudly several times round the parade square, smartly saluting, presenting arms, turning right, left and about as we demonstrated to our loved ones what a shower of shit – sorry, what a well-oiled, well-disciplined, well-petrified part of Her Majesty's defence we had incredibly become in such a short time!

Afterwards we were released back into the community, back to from whence we had come, *for a short period of rejoicing*, as Churchill had said at the end of the Second World War, before being sent onward for trade training. My only memory of this all-too-brief interlude, apart from the fact that my little brother had commandeered my bedroom immediately I was away, was that it became apparent that my language had taken a decided turn for the worse. This was brutally exposed as soon as I was safely back within the bosom of my family.

From a lad who would previously blush if anyone said 'bloody' or even worse 'bugger' in public, things had quickly taken a step backwards; the language of the forces had got to me. Around the family dinner table on my first evening home I was recounting a story about when we were camping in Sherwood Forest, when my sister innocently asked if it was cold there. I will never forget the aghast look on my mother's face, as I helpfully offered the following fully explanatory and descriptive phrase.

'It was fuggin' freezing, Alison. I nearly froze my bollocks off!'

My father, normally the verbal disciplinarian of the family, but with a lifelong hearing problem (which I later inherited), looked somewhat puzzled, as if he didn't quite understand, or believe what I had said. There was a numb silence before someone changed the subject.

Later I mumbled an apology to my mother, who said 'Don't you ever let your father hear you say *that* word!' – which I found confusing. Which word? And I was doubtful as to Dad's actions if I did use it. He had plenty to say when he hit his thumb instead of a nail with the hammer.

So, at the age of just under eighteen, my language was changed forever. More positively I was now fitter than ever before or since in my life and I was growing, both up in height and out in stature, and becoming a man as I left home, really for good.

I was on my way!

7. A Hard Day's Night

Any weekday – we didn't work weekends – at 7 am-ish, in our crewroom, you would find two kinds of airmen. These could be both officially and visually differentiated by two clear aspects: marriage and appearance. The *scalies*, a slang term for married men (officially m/fs, meaning *married with families*) were in general a bit smarter and certainly cleaner in terms of hygiene and would be more likely to be wearing an ironed shirt. Most even wore ties to work. But the *singles*, of which I was a fully-paid-up member, were, almost to a man scruffier and more hirsute. It would be fifty/fifty as to whether their chins had seen a razor that morning. In truth, the actual time they had been out of their beds that morning would have been measured in minutes, rather than one or two hours, like the scalies, the latter no doubt having been serviced and breakfasted by their wives. These adoring women – mostly, anyway – would care how their husband looked as he went off to serve his Queen and Country.

Their appearance was in sharp contrast to we uncossetted singles, who had to provide our own version of the uniform we were required to wear. Cold weather gear was favoured most of the year, because it hid many blemishes. This consisted of a cavernous waterproof anorak thing with a big hood (apparently it was originally designed as naval-issue to work on the decks of aircraft carriers), this then covering a big, loose, heavy-duty dark blue crew-neck jumper, worn over a collarless (and probably un-ironed) shirt. Below the waist, regulation thick, coarse, serge-blue trousers were worn and for footwear 'Trog' boots – big heavy rubber affairs – were worn. Smart, eh?

The laugh was that in the apple-picking season, i.e. late summer/early autumn, such sartorially-dressed airmen like me, apart from the coarse trousers, used Her Majesty's uniform to pick apples in. The Queen's uniform was ideal for muddy long grass and going up and down ladders amongst the branches, it was suitable even if it was summer. All you had to do when coming back from a day's apple-picking was have your tea, change your trousers and go to work, having earned some money – great! Although a minority did care about how they looked at work (including picking apples), the majority, including me, didn't give a rat's. It was far from high on our list of priorities. Absolutely no-one at work took any notice of such matters as appearance, as long as you wore some kind of uniform and you did your job satisfactorily.

Some singlies made an early visit to the mess for a greasy breakfast, after all it was five and a half hours until lunchtime. Any single airman had become accustomed to eating food most people would have turned their nose up at in a café. Other hardy specimens preferred the fags-and-coffee type of *petit-dejeuner* at work in the crewroom. These were usually those who spent more than enough evening time in pubs during the week, indulging in late-night throwing-out time visits to the chippy, where the favourite meal seemed to be not fish and chips but a heavily-spiced local version of faggots with chips. The 'downside' – particularly apt – was the catastrophic wind-effect of the said faggots the morning after. Not to put too fine a point on it, it was very unwise to be positioned near such offenders in early morning.

So in addition to appearances, you associated singlies, especially first thing in the morning, with halitosis, belching, farting (in some cases unbelievably smelly), suspect hygiene and usually bad temper or at least monosyllabic grunts until mid-morning. By contrast, the scalies were almost human. Some of them didn't live in married quarters, they lived off camp and had to travel in daily. This entailed coming into contact with the general public, unlike singlies, thus necessitating basic grooming of some sort. Of course there was good-natured banter between the two divisions, most scalies being of the poacher-turned-gamekeeper variety, no strangers to such scant personal attention experienced in an earlier life whilst single.

Aircraft needed to be made ready before they could fly and our heavier friends, the riggers (airframes) and engines were usually out doing heavily whatever they did, grunting and swearing as they went about it. But before aircraft can go anywhere, they have to be 'seen-off', and as fairies, i.e the lighter (more intelligent?) trades with lesser workloads, we were favourite for such duties as seeing-off aircraft. This was a two-man job. A visit to the stores enabled collection of two sets of ear-defenders (large linked plastic half-egg shaped items worn over each ear to protect one from the considerable noise) plus two large fluorescent bats to *marshal the aircraft* (i.e. signal to the pilot) the direction to taxi in.

You would arrive at the designated plane on its concrete pan and remove the four large, yellow, wooden chocks on either side of the huge main wheels under the fuselage. From somewhere, left around from the last one, you would wheel a two-cylinder fire extinguisher over to the vicinity immediately in front of the port wing... and wait. The quartermaster would eventually come out with his headset on, connected by a long lead to the inside intercom and he was your link, by visual signals, to the captain inside. One by one, the huge propellers would roar into life. I never saw one catch fire but one of you manned the fire extinguishers just in case. When all were running ok, the quartermaster would nod and climb in, shutting the door behind him.

One of you would then stand under the nose, holding the two ropes that were attached to the nose-wheel chocks. Your partner would have the marshalling bats (these were replaced by lighted wands after dark) and take up position well in front of the aircraft, where the captain on the right of the flight deck, facing you, could see you. On the that signal he was ready to go, the batman indicated to the other incumbent to remove the nose-wheel chocks; these would be dragged away off the pans onto the nearby grass. The main brake was released and the huge Hercules would slowly begin to creep forward, marshalled off the pan onto the peri-track (perimeter road) that led round to the runways. To marshal the aircraft, the heavy fluorescent bats were raised up and down together to signal to the captain to move forward; together meant straight ahead; one fixed, the other up and down meant turning towards whichever way was fixed; the speed of the bats indicated the recommended trundling speed. Crossing the bats overhead meant stop, the speed of doing so a clue to the urgency required to stop!

To see the aircraft back safely in, the opposite scenario then applied. One of the shift controllers would come into the crewroom and assess the casual scene in front of him. Using a combination of cunning, insider-knowledge, devilment or whatever, he would call out to two likely suspects, something like:

'Mac, Justin – go and see 184 into pan six, will you?'

Depending on the card game/darts/coffee/chat/whatever, the response was usually grudgingly casual acceptance of some sort, and off you went to the stores to get the said equipment. Fairly early on, I learnt a valuable lesson from one of the old-timers – that such jobs took up valuable boring work time. A great deal of the time working around aircraft was spent just waiting around for something to happen, hence the experienced card-sharps and/or deadly dart-players. By almost volunteering – looking up brightly usually worked – one got most of those mundane jobs going, two or three of which, lasting about thirty to forty-five minutes each, soon passed a morning or afternoon. Combined with a few servicings, i.e. those vital checks made on every aircraft before and after they flew, and you had a day's work. These servicing checks were b/f's – before flights, a/f's – after flights, af/bf's – the two combined, and turn-rounds, a check made where the aircraft came down, but was to take off again shortly.

The long day shift finished at four thirty. I always thought this unfair as one started at seven, having to do five and a half long hours until lunch at twelve thirty, plus three hours in the afternoon, which is why I always plumped for the unpopular 'earlies' shift. This is where a skeleton crew came in at five am (yes, I was often still pissed when I came in at that hour!) but finished for the day at twelve thirty.

All this day activity, however, was markedly different to the night shift, which was great. I loved 'nights'. Having come into work at four thirty, there was a certain briskness in the air to get the work done as, with absolutely no exceptions, we all knew as soon as the work was finished we could all go home: scalies back to wives, children-where-applicable, TV, or whatever scalies did, singlies usually to who-knows-where? Of course, a lot depended on what that actual finishing time was, but sometimes an early finish could mean an unplanned sortie to some fun-palace, with sometimes some unplanned fun.

Of course money, or lack of it, dictated a great deal of activity or otherwise. One couldn't afford seven days a week going out on the razz, although some tried. In our little circle, we tended to hit the scene at weekends, mostly the plan was like the working man's life in civvy street, where we would get pissed locally on a Friday night; Saturday night was 'Big Night Out' on the razz to clubs like the Kontiki or the Beach Club on Hayling Island, a 'Mecca Run' in Portsmouth to celebrate anything worth celebrating, or parties in (well-known) haunts like the nurses home in Chichester Hospitals or wherever rich pickings could be found. Sundays tended to be more sedate; sometimes at the classy 'Bali-Hai' club at Pagham near Bognor Regis, or a quiet night out somewhere. Sundays were usually reserved for taking girls out rather than trying to pick them up and endeavouring to inspect their underwear and everything inside it, in the back of a car usually. Although, come to think of it, the 'end' intention was actually the same, albeit 'attacked' in a different way. How did I get on to sex from talking about nights? Oh yes, what we got up to some evenings when we finished work early.

A great place to relax in was our very own Sailing Club, over the far side of the island. It was a large modern building with a huge lounge window giving a panoramic view of the bay. One of my huge regrets in life is not learning to sail under those conditions, the unabashed truth is there always seemed something more important to do at the Club: be it women, drinking or music – sorry I mean wine, women and song! 'Discos' were just coming in, there was a turntable deck thing there and we had more than one budding DJ in our midst, although strangely enough the biggest wanker of that lot unbelievably made it right through to the BBC, via local Portsmouth radio, when leaving the RAF shortly after I did. There is another story there, which I won't record now, but it involves him...

Oh yes, we made use of the Sailing Club in many ways. Some nights after finishing early we would make our way over there, some people would take their evening meal break in the Club; liquid of course, they didn't do food. So you could enter in uniform, nobody cared; although strictly speaking it was supposed to be civilian dress as the public also came in, but they were supposed to be signed in by a member. We were all automatic members as serving airmen. So, as ever where drink is concerned, you finished early enough, say eight-thirty, popped into the Club for a pint to relax after work – and ended up drunk by closing time! It wasn't always good for your pocket and head the next morning when you finished early on nights...

8.   When I'm Cleaning Windows

One day Justin and I were sitting in the crew room as usual, drinking coffee, as usual, waiting for something to happen, as usual. Justin was a fascinating character, I'll tell you why another time. We shared a room together with eight other incumbents, but Justin and I had the two corner beds farthest from the door, which were on the end wall of the long narrow room. We were also on the same shift at work, our trades (the actual type of work we did) were adjacent, so on this occasion we were seen as a pair.

Sid Oldridge sidled up to us, slyly looking to left and right as he approached, as though he was being watched. He was the nearest thing to a spiv you could get in the RAF at that time, he reminded you of Private Walker in *Dad's Army*. Anything devious or underhanded he always knew about: cheap fags, booze, which horse was going to win the three-thirty at Chepstow that afternoon, that sort of thing. He looked and acted the part with lank, greasy, mousy-coloured hair curling over his collar; a scruffy moustache added to the generally underhand appearance. Sid was as skinny as a rake with a permanent cigarette hanging from the corner of his mouth, an amount of ash always dangling precariously from the end. He glanced quickly at the door, as though the police were about to burst in and raid the place at any second.

'You lads interested in making some extra cash?' he muttered, speaking out of the non-fag side of his mouth, making it sound highly illegal. Well, in those days we were up for almost anything to make any extra cash: wine, women and song were not cheaply available on the South Coast in the late sixties. So yes, of course we were interested!

Sid had an entrepreneurial streak in him; it later transpired that a recent section do, a sort of official services party where wives and girlfriends were invited, Sid was chatting to one of the m/fs wives. One particular wife dropped into the conversation that she was fed up with cleaning her own windows because there was no window cleaner on the married quarters on our camp.

Now to most people that would not have registered, but to Sid it was like a one-armed bandit where the bells were lining up. He immediately started asking round, checking out the facts, and realised he had a potential winner on his hands. By the time he approached Justin and I, he had done a tour round the married quarters, knocking on doors, asking who would like their windows cleaned, suggesting a fee, and coming away with a list of addresses and an agreed price.

From somewhere in his vast contact list of dodgy characters, Sid then borrowed a set of ladders – I said he was an entrepreneur – then actually, from his own pocket I think (hard to believe) purchased two buckets, two chamois leathers and two sponges. From somewhere buried in his vast encyclopaedia of life's knowledge, Sid knew exactly how to clean windows, and instructed us accordingly. He had also been over to the other side of the airfield to the hallowed Officers Married Quarters, where much bigger houses meant much bigger charges and much bigger profits!

Justin and I started work the following Monday in springtime as we were on nights that week. On the part of the station where we worked, a two-shift system operated. The total work force was split into two, one section working days from seven am to four thirty pm, the night shift then coming in to take over at four-thirty. The night shift then worked until all had been done and finished properly, which could theoretically mean virtually any time between six pm and five am the next day, when an early day shift skeleton crew arrived to get the aircraft ready for a normal day. The two shifts alternated every week, so you worked a week of days, then followed by a week of nights, etc.

Sid had organised our payment structure as follows: a standard terraced house on the airmens' married quarters was charged at twenty-five pence. We each received ten pence, and five pence went to 'The Business'; the total of the five pences being paid to Sid at the end of each working day at tea-time before Justin and I went on the night shift. As this was springtime, it could be hard work, up and down the ladders all day, usually in bright sunshine there on the South Coast. As the summer months came we were invariably cream-crackered by the time we really went to work officially in the late afternoon.

Now at this point, I would like to tell you something; you might already have anticipated what I am going to say if you have ever been in the Forces. Servicemen always tend to look for the quick and easy way to do virtually anything, and there is inevitably one to be found. In our case, knowing Sid and the way he worked was a huge advantage. When he himself was on nights his normal daily routine was to get out of bed late, say tennish (nice for some), his lifestyle embraced the 'fags and coffee' type of breakfast while reading 'The Sporting Life' or the racing pages of the tabloids, before catching the eleven or eleven-thirty bus off the camp into the local town.

For the next four to five hours Sid would alternate between the betting shop and the local pubs (there were in excess of twenty pubs in the local town at that time, I remember), before catching the three fifteen or three forty-five bus back to camp. Suitably well-oiled, and either in pleasant post-winning bliss (he knew his horseracing) or alternatively anxious to receive some much-needed replenishment funds, he would immediately accept whatever we gave him without checking, stuffing it in his pocket before anyone could see or query it, although no-one ever did. Sid never queried anything, I'm sure he just saw it as extra cash for himself, no questions asked.

I would say by the end of the first day we had it all sussed. Justin was older and wiser than me, and knew all the dodges: yes, agreed, we were grateful for Sid's initiative in giving us the opportunity to earn some much-needed extra cash – but no, we weren't prepared to work our goolies off all day and meekly hand over the correctly-due amount to Sid, while he passed his day doing exactly the opposite.

Yes, yes – I know that's not the correct way to look at it, but as I said, this was the services and it doesn't work like that, ask anyone who's been in. I'm sure Sid was aware of precisely what we actually did, and he would have done exactly the same in our place. Justin and I worked backwards financially, by paying Sid exactly what would be the very minimum expected of us, and taking it from there. Once we had earned 'The Business's due amount in hard cash, i.e. x houses at five pence = y, we separated that off to give to Sid later, then everything we earned from then on was ours. At the end of the day we split the money fifty-fifty and everyone was happy: the only trouble was some evenings after finishing nights early, we were too shattered to go out and spend our money, but hey ho, it was all very welcome.

A few notable incidents occurred while in the pursuit of our window cleaning duties. One blistering day we were over at the posh end of the island, the Officers Married Quarters, and I was round the back of one particular mansion, a Wing Commander's house. I put my ladder on the paved patio in front of the closed French windows and mounted the ladder to clean the large bedroom window directly above. Below, I heard someone open the French windows and the sounds of a deckchair being assembled.

By the time I came down, all I could see was the two opened pages of *The Daily Telegraph*, two dainty hands, and the bottom torso of a woman sitting on the deckchair. I bent down to wash my leathers etc, only to be able to see straight up the said woman's skirts, invitingly open it seemed. I would like to quickly add, in my defence, that at the time, unlike today, I was a lusty, single nineteen-year-old with testosterone raging through my arteries – everywhere, and the sight of her virginally white knickers, white thighs and stocking tops, went directly – well not to my head exactly, but to another part of my anatomy; in my fashionably-short brief shorts, I could not stand (?) up, as my inflamed situation would be obvious and perhaps even curtail my career.

For what seemed hours, probably only minutes, I vigorously rinsed my leathers, looked elsewhere, and concentrated hard on (should I use that phrase?) whether Chelsea would beat Leeds in the forthcoming Cup Final. Football usually works, should the situation arise! Eventually I managed to limply stand up, only to come face to face with my tormentor. I was greatly taken aback to find without the newspaper cover she appeared older than my mother, a tad 'twinset and pearls' with greying hair, and I blushed beetroot red as she smiled politely and paid me, even giving me a tip (I know, don't keep looking up older ladies skirts!).

A bonus from the window cleaning was that while doing it, I did actually meet a girl called Lesley, a daughter of one of the senior airman – fortunately not one I knew at work – and we kind of dated for a short while. I say 'kind of' because nothing memorably physical happened between us, not for want of trying on my part of course, but I do remember two things about her. One is that she was the worst kisser I can ever remember, on impact her lips disappeared into her mouth and you found you were impaled on her skin and gums, not a pleasant experience. The other is that our special record together was *This Old Heart of Mine* by *The Isley Brothers*; we played it incessantly as we grappled away on her parents' sofa while they were out. Even hearing it again today always brings back the married quarters, window cleaning and trying to work out how to tell Lesley about improving her kissing technique (I never did!).

I think the window cleaning lasted about six months before the apple-picking season started again; now that was a money spinner not to be missed, and not such hard physical work. For some reason we could never fathom, we were paid by the hour, not by what we picked! No prizes for guessing we spun it out much longer than it should have! Justin and I gave our notice in to Sid, who promptly recruited two more hungry young money-seekers and continued his debauched activities; needless to say we did not pass on our *modus operandi* – I'm sure being servicemen they worked out their own!

The last thing I heard of Sid, he was in civvy street, selling Rolls-Royce cars in Weybridge, Surrey. Sid could sell sand to the Arabs if he set his mind to it. I have no doubt that he probably is, as we speak. Altogether now... 'When I'm cleaning windows...'

Move over, George Formby!

9.   El Adem

The Hooray-Henry woman behind me on the barstool was older than me by about twenty years, married but 'fancied herself', if you know what I mean. She loved being in the bar after work with the men, flirting and playing games with some, although I think most of us regarded her as a pain in the arse. I know I did. But this particular evening something she was saying and the way she was saying it got right up my nose. The year was 1975, three years after my RAF career had ended, but some of it was still vivid. This bit was etched in my memory banks under 'P' for Painful.

As far as I was concerned, the name was simply pronounced as written – 'El Adem' – to rhyme with to 'tell madam'. But when Teresa Merry pronounced it, the *Ad* was pronounced, dragged out and stressed, as in *Ard*, with 'em' using the Arabic pronunciation to make it sound oriental and mystical. She was telling her audience in the bar about this fabulously exotic place with its far-eastern name, making it sound like a jewel of the East, a very sociable and desirable place to live in, in married military officers land, where life was one big gay whirl of cocktail parties, social fun, the mess, dancing, drinking and high living.

Well, that didn't sound like the El Adem I knew and loathed. As far as I, and a considerable number of other Royal Air Force airmen were concerned, El Adem was the pits, the arsehole of the world (after Aden apparently, which was worse, so the old lags told me). From a single serviceman's point of view, this staging/refuelling post eighteen miles inland from Second World War ravaged Tobruk in the Libyan desert was a living nightmare; it had absolutely had nothing going for it. Quite simply, the food was awful, the accommodation disgusting, working conditions extremely difficult due to the searing dry heat and leisure facilities almost nil. What a place!

Most foreign postings in unpleasant places were only one year's duration. Using a combination of knuckling down and studying for one's next promotional exam and saving a considerable amount of money (i.e. little to spend it on), a year away had its advantages: but El Adem was totally wrong. Somebody had badly deemed it a two-year tour, and it was said that a number of young airmen could not accept this horrible shock to the system and committed suicide while there as a result. This was a well-kept secret, but in reality it was simply that bad – so when I heard this pampered woman portraying the place as some kind of paradisiacal oasis of service life I could not keep quiet.

Unusually for me, I asked her outright if she knew how many airmen had taken their own lives living in the squalid, fearsomely hot conditions, eating the rubbish food, with constant stomach complaints as a result, being bitten by the horrible insects that exist in Libya, mainly due to sleeping in accommodation known as 'the stables'. There was absolutely sod-all of any real value to do with your time. For single men there were absolutely no women in Libya, some were even pathetically reduced to sniffing seats on aircraft passing through where females had sat, dreaming of another world they had forfeited when they signed on, never dreaming life could be as awful and uncivilised as this. I was there briefly three times in the supposedly 'swinging' sixties in 1968 and 1969, fortunately only on detachment for three weeks at a time, but long enough to experience and remember its horrors with a shudder.

Apparently, some years before, in the early sixties, a group of single airmen revolted at El Adem, complaining bitterly about the disgusting state of the food, collecting the slops served and putting it straight into the dustbins to make their point. I have never actually heard of any other similarly organized protest in the normally sophisticated Royal Air Force, so this must have taken some doing – it even reached Parliament back in the UK and questions were asked. Well, apparently, the strong protest worked for a while, fresh milk was even flown in from Malta, but all I can say is that by the time I reached there in 1968 it had reverted to pigswill: the worst food I had ever tasted. I remember they even had a steak bar in the mess, you queued up for ages to get a wizened piece of meat that looked and tasted like shoe leather.

As if the food wasn't bad enough, the accommodation was appalling. You were housed in miserable-looking single storey Nissan-type huts, reminiscent of the things you see in wartime prison camps, a la *Stalag 44*. You entered at one end and walked between two lines of dark, forbidding closely-packed, narrow bunk-beds either side, with a single very narrow walk-way down the middle; each room held about sixty men, with absolutely no privacy whatsoever. This was my first time abroad as a serviceman and what a revelation it was – so this was how Her Majesty's government treated its forces overseas, some twenty-three years after the end of a monumental war – did we really win it? Why wasn't anything being done? Surely prisoners were treated better than this?

When I first stepped off the plane in Libya, I just could not believe the heat, it simply took your breath away. But this was a different heat to, say, Spain, the only place abroad I had ever been to. Libya was totally dry, the hot wind seemed to go straight through you, taking the moisture, leaving you drained and tired. You just could not, and were advised strongly not to, spend very long out in it, or you would pay the price of rapid dehydration.

Leisure pursuits were limited to table tennis, a Scalextric model car racing club – little boys toys to me – a local radio station and a must, especially for all newcomers – a trip to Tobruk. On my first detachment to El Adem I duly boarded the ramshackle old bus, which lumbered out of the camp gates to start the dusty eighteen mile route; a dead straight dusty track road to the coast through the desert. 'Desert' sounds Arabic, mystical, exciting, perhaps evoking images of beautiful sandy scenery and palm trees. Well, Libya in reality was nothing like this at all. The scenery was sandy-coloured all right but littered with boulders and scrubland wherever you looked. It appeared very unappealing and unforgiving.

Suddenly without warning we passed a huge square grey concrete building, like a fortress or well-built prison: not displeasing to the eye, but not really attractive either. On enquiring we were told that this was the Commonwealth War Cemetery, and if we looked out of the opposite window we would shortly see the German one. Following my previous comments about how we treat our armed forces I should have known, because this was some building to look at, and easily put ours to shame: bright, shining, a fitting monument to the dead. As a serving member of those forces charged with the defence of the realm, I have always been struck by the fact that one day I might be called to lay down my life for my country and if the need arose I would do my duty. There are no good places to die for your country, whether on land, sea or air, but I cannot think of a worse place to die than Libya, and my heart goes out to those who did – there can be no greater sacrifice.

Tobruk appeared to be as if the war had just finished; buildings were half-fallen down, the streets were dusty and dirty, with hardly anyone about. We went to the one good place, the beach, where the turquoise blue-green waters of the magical Mediterranean were as clear as could possibly be. Like many other servicemen before us over the years, my mates and I frolicked happily there for a while. Later, while strolling back through the deserted, run-down streets, three of us found ourselves in a little tourist shop, selling souvenirs, manned by a small Arab boy. On arriving at the knives section, we discovered an alarming array of vicious flick-knives, those favoured by Teddy-boys in Britain in the 50s and early 60s. Taking turns to frighten each other with the biggest one we could find, we suddenly realised the mechanism wasn't working correctly. We immediately tried to 'lose' it, but we reckoned without a huge Arab suddenly blocking our path, replacing the boy and who now heavily demanded payment for the knife.

It is always drummed into servicemen abroad not to fall out with the locals, especially those of us only here on detachment, so we had a rapid bargaining session with Abdul, followed by a whip-round. It seemed to be the most expensive item in the whole shop! Now the proud possessors of a huge dodgy flick-knife, we debated for hours what to do with it, as our customs would be decidedly unimpressed if they discovered it in our luggage. But like all good groundcrew, we had our own hiding places on our aircraft, depending on one's individual trade. In the end, one of our units of radio equipment flew back to the UK minus an air filter, no harm done. In its place was the now-repaired knife, fully functional. Back home we then approached McGovern, the local Scottish hardman and misfit in our midst, who was always in trouble with the law, both military and civil, and sold him the knife, making a good profit. Last thing I heard, McGovern was discharged ignominiously (i.e. thrown out). I hope it wasn't for knife-related crimes...

One day while on duty in Libya, very bored while the planes were flying, we decided to have a scorpion hunt. We spread out into the 'bondu' – a forces word meaning the desert – to carefully hunt for our prey. I was actually watching one of our number, a big individual who was turning over a large rock, when he screamed and jumped a foot in the air. He hadn't been bitten but the sight of this evil-looking little creature made everyone jump and when it moved – boy, I've never see grown men shift so fast!

At times like this, there is always some smart-arse who knows it all. It was suggested we find another scorpion, make a circle of petrol-soaked rope on the ground, put the two scorpions in the circle, light the rope and they would fight to the death. So went the theory. There were a few snags here. First, we only had one scorpion – we were hunting for another when we got news the aircraft were returning shortly and work called. Problem – what to do with the one we've got ? Cue know-it-all duty smart-arse, that if we 'stunned it' – with Carbon Tetrachloride (CTC) from any fire extinguisher found in MT vehicles, we could knock it out, to be played with later. After much dangerous baiting and prodding with sticks, time running out and much cowardly running away when the tiny scorpion moved the wrong way, we managed to get the dear little creature into a clear plastic bag.

There was one further problem though. Shortly after fire extinguishers containing CTC were issued to all MT vehicles it was discovered that the product was excellent for removing stains: consequently when one was actually required to put out a fire, there was no CTC in it, although everyone around's uniform was spotless. To get round this, a bright red dye was put in with the CTC, so with several heroes holding the plastic bag on the end of sticks, someone fired the red CTC into the plastic bag, only for the poor scorpion to go mad (well you would, wouldn't you?). It obviously killed the poor little bugger, so we had a very short requiem mass out in the *bondu*, just in time for the planes returning. Well... it passed a few bored hours one hot afternoon.

After I had done three detachments in El Adem, a sudden course of political events in Libya changed everything, both for me and more meaningfully for a lot of other RAF servicemen. The old pro-British King Idris died, his weak young son took over and was abruptly overthrown in a military coup. The leader of the uprising? Why, one Colonel Gaddafi, who hated the British and promptly threw them all out – hurray! It certainly saved the sanity – and perhaps lives – of a lot of young servicemen, and for me meant that future detachments took me to the real Mediterranean – to Cyprus, Gibraltar and Malta, the former particularly I grew to love. Malta was fine too, and Gib – in fact anywhere was better than El Adem!

British servicemen are a tough, stoical breed. They put up with some awful conditions in some terrible places in the world, both in the past, today and no doubt in the future. In the main, they are uncomplaining and just get on with the job. But I know a shit-hole when I see one and, as you can see, I am still twitchy when I hear the name 'El Adem', because of the terrific jolt to the system it gave me at the time.

I certainly punctured Teresa Merry's happy tales of her idyllic life in the Middle East. I bet she hated Gaddafi for what he did in throwing out the British. But I didn't!

10. Cracking the Mess

'Will you shut up, you fugging morons!' They were giggling so much, so uncontrollably I felt sure someone would hear. Both my mates Steve and Dave had got the giggles, we were all pissed but we were also ravenous – and trying to break into our mess to get something to eat in the middle of the night. We had hit on this novel idea a few days earlier, as we were always coming in from a boozing session starving hungry – a night's ale always does that for some reason. These were the days before twenty-four hour catering, Ronald McDonald was just another Scotsman and you were lucky to find a chippie open later than 10.30. The late sixties was the dark ages catering-wise. Fast food had not yet been invented – only slow get-it-where-you-can food was sporadically available.

So someone – it might even have been me – had this brainwave. There were three big sash windows along the front wall of the dining room of the mess, illuminated by the streetlights outside, but a similar one at the side was in near darkness at night. By sitting by that window at tea one afternoon it was relatively easy to slide the lock out of place so the window could be eased up from outside. Now here we were, actually trying to do it, except for the idiots I was with, pissing themselves laughing while I tried to quietly slide the window up.

Mancunian Dave was absolutely useless, sobbing paralytically flat on his back on the manicured grass and out of it. I swore at Steve so much that he idiotically gave me such an unnecessary shove upwards I crashed straight over the window sill and fell onto the shiny parquet floor of our dining hall, not that I could see anything, it was pitch black.

'Stay here and SHUT UP' I hissed to Morecambe and Wise. 'I'm going to see what I can find'. There were several problems. Our actual mess, the large room we all ate in, was only part of the place. There was a long, stainless-steel servery, where we queued up to receive our food from sour-faced civilian cooks. Behind them were two huge double swing doors to the kitchens, although we had never been in there, so I had no idea of the geography of the place. I climbed over the servery and crept through the swing doors into the kitchen. All around there were huge cooking ovens, grills, hot plates, etc, but I had no idea whatsoever where any food would be stored. Presumably, there were industrial-sized fridges, freezers, storage larders, whatever – but where?

Of course, I daren't show any lights. The guardroom was a couple of hundred yards away, diagonally across the car park – sorry, parade square – and any lights of any sort could be spotted easily. So it was totally in-the-dark stuff. An army pongo (private) would have found it easily, they were trained for things like this, in the dark. My vital role in first-line aircraft servicing, involving radio black-box changing, didn't help a bit.

It was like being on a *Doctor Who* set when everyone had gone home, huge lifeless machines everywhere – where were the Daleks? In the darkness I could see there was a door at the back leading away down a passage, so I quietly opened it. I suddenly felt scared – I could end up in the glasshouse for this. As I'd always got away with everything dodgy before, I didn't want to start a naughty tab now.

Off this passage were two or three doors either side with a big metal fire-door facing me at the end, I assumed this was the outer one. One door revealed a cloakroom-cum-bathroom affair next to the back door, another big metal door was locked: it could have been a cold store I thought. Inside the other was a square room, along the sides I could just make out some racks, on which I found... some loaves of sliced bread! At the end of the racks, across one end of the room was what seemed to be a huge industrial type fridge, like one of those American 'Kelvinator' affairs you see on *Happy Days* that could feed an army – well, an Air Force, at least. Trouble was, I couldn't open it. The bloody thing seemed to have no handle on it in the dark. So near, yet so far. For what seemed like ages, I ran my hands over it, feeling like a novice safe-breaker where no-one's told me the secret code.

I heard a distant crash and muffled swearing. Going back up the passage, I saw the shape of my mate Steve bumping into the ovens and hot plates in the kitchen, making a noise.

'Shut up! What the fug are you doing?'

'Avn't you found anything yet – I'm starving!' he moaned.

'Come here and show me how you open this.' I took him into the room and showed him Metal Mayzi, expecting him to be flummoxed like me. Blow me if he didn't walk straight up, put his hand up to the top, grabbed a huge handle that ran across the unit, pulled it down and the big door swung invitingly open – and a light came on!

It was a bit like finding Tutankhamen's tomb, except that instead of mummified remains we found – food, loads of it. There were trays of eggs, large catering packs of bacon and sausages, packs of butter, blocks of cheese, catering packs of mayonnaise, coleslaw and... a part-carved pork joint. Now what? Where do we go from here? We held a summit meeting, lasting all of thirty seconds. We took a loaf of bread, a pack of butter, a slab of cheese, and guess what else? Oh yes, the pork joint. Nicking a couple of plates from the clean piles of several thousand, we piled our ill-gotten gains up and handed the lot through the window to our sobering-up and starving Mancunian mate. Back in Steve's 'bunk' – being a corporal Steve had his own tiny room – we had our own midnight feast.

Stolen fruit had never tasted so good!

Now, of course the question was, who do we share our new secret with? We had a circle of about ten of us who knocked about together and an inner sanctum of about six, who we told the next day. For a couple of further months we regularly 'cracked the mess' when we came back starving from boozy nights out and took pot luck at whatever there was there. But good news travels and drink talks. One night Steve and I came back hungry and. as usual, as I was smaller and lighter, Steve nudged me over the threshold. But I was very quiet that night...

As I silently approached the servery, through the swing doors I could see our mate Geordie, he of The Twins fame (see Chapter 22). As if in a cartoon, he was idiotically tiptoeing rapidly around the kitchen, busy as a bee. He had the temerity – or bollocks, whichever you prefer – to have lit the huge hob and was actually frying eggs in the biggest frying pan I have ever seen. For a second or two I watched transfixed. Geordie's sheer cheek astounded me. It had never occurred to me – or us – to actually *cook* anything in the mess. I negotiated my way silently over the servery and crept up to the swing doors, suddenly crashing through them.

'Hey! What the fugginell's going on'ere then?'

Geordie nearly shit himself with fright.

'Jesus, Mac, don't do that! Fancy a fried egg sandwich?' he said, swiftly recovering his equilibrium. I had to laugh. Geordie had style, as well as cheek. Laid out neatly were twelve slices of bread and butter, and the six eggs were crackling away in the Sunday School frying pan.

'Are you hungry, Geordie?' I asked enviously at the sight of this gastronomic feast. There was more fat on a chip than skinny old Geordie, he was like a whippet on a diet.

'No, I only want one myself,' he replied, quick as a flash. 'But I've taken orders in my block at a quid each, made myself a fiver – but you can have one for nowt. How do you like your eggs?' I took two for Steve and I and left gratefully – good old Geordie!

One night Steve and I picked up a couple of girls. We thought they 'might', so we decided to come clean and tell them we were in the RAF for once. Because we brought them back onto camp with us, we had to tell them. It's difficult to convince young women you're an IBM computer engineer when you live on a RAF station and have short hair. Anyway, Steve was starving, as usual, so were they, they said, so we left them in Steve's bunk and cracked the mess. You should have seen their faces when we arrived with half a cooked chicken, a sliced loaf and a pack of butter. We all tucked in and enjoyed the rough chicken sandwiches, so after investing earlier in several halves of lager, we had now dined them as well as wining them.

So now to other pleasures... Sadly, I lived in a room with five other blokes, but it was a challenge to woo mine separately into bed. Not surprisingly, I failed, but not without some success along the way. I quietly took her into my communal room in the dark, shushing her along. It was the early hours and although we did have a promising grapple and grope on the bed for a while, just when things were getting a bit steamy she heard snoring, then farting and realized we were not alone! That put an end to that, but after re-adjusting our clothing, as we crept out of the room to find out what was happening elsewhere, a northern voice was heard from a distant corner. 'Night, love!' it said. My efforts had not gone unnoticed. As it happened, Steve wasn't getting things all his own way either in his bunk, but for different reasons. His told him in no uncertain terms she wasn't doing it 'on the first night' – so that was that. There was never going to be a second night in those days and we took them home.

But it was a funny old night – and a great laugh the next day.

Soon our secret was out and, of course, our days of 'cracking the mess' were numbered, it was only a question of time. We were careful for the next few months but things came to a head one night, although fortunately no-one got caught. We had a head-banging Scotsman (there were a few of those) in our midst called Billy McAteer, a good lad to have on your side, especially playing football, but he had his wild moments, especially around drink. This night he was on his own, well-pissed, and the stupid bugger switched the lights on in the mess to get his bearings. An eagle-eyed RAF policeman, perhaps tipped off with rumours abounding of hungry late-night diners and thieves, saw the light and came over to investigate. He hammered on the big front door of the mess, looked in the windows and inside Billy panicked.

The copper came round the side, saw the open window and flashed his torch inside, shouting to whoever to give themselves up. Billy sneaked through to the back and managed to break out via a tiny window in the cloakroom and got away – Scot-free? But we were rumbled. The cooks had, of course, begun to notice their disappearing stocks and had started asking questions.

'Cracking the Mess' was a few months of fun while it lasted and had fed us royally on a few notable occasions.

11. Women!

I suppose, if I am honest, most of my serious leisure activities during my five years in the RAF involved chasing young women, usually involving alcohol. The long, hot summer I arrived at RAF Thorney Island on the South Coast near Portsmouth was the year of flower power, peace and love. One old hand told us newly-arrived horny young airmen, just out of training, that we should head straight for the local 'Mecca', the dance hall in the centre of Portsmouth, where, he said, 'if you can't get a girl there, you should shoot yourself!' Armed with this important piece of information, we set sail for this apparent El Dorado of lovelies to seek our fortune.

What was on offer, however, was not quite as available – or attractive – as we had been led to believe, and our short hair stood out a mile. I should add at this point that the very, very last thing we ever admitted to was being in the services. Everyone knows Portsmouth is the home of the Royal Navy, and we did not want to be tarred – tarred, get it? – with that association, so we would lie through our teeth to girls we met that we were absolutely anything but a military serviceman. Computer programmer was a favourite (IBM was nearby), footballers (unlikely if you saw us play), HGV drivers (but only of dangerous chemicals naturally, not your run-of-the-mill versions) and when you got carried away by drink, which was frequently – chicken psychologists – i.e. to persuade chickens by scientific means – light, heat, colours etc – to lay brown eggs rather than white. Most of the more gullible swallowed it, a straight face was needed for this – six pints would usually suffice!

I went to the Mecca one night with a staunch Yorkshireman, Phil from Doncaster (Donneh!), proud of it of course, with strong accent to match. We were dancing with two local girls, trying to chat them up, and I overheard his beauty saying to him.

'Ay – you don't 'alf talk fanny (sic), where are you from?'

'God's coontreh!' he announced boldly.

'Ooh,' she replied. 'Are you a Jew?'

I collapsed laughing but he, she and my lovely didn't think it was 'fanny' at all! Needless to say, it all came to nothing, as did many trips to the Mecca. We had much more success elsewhere. Without wishing to sound too middle-class, the sort of girls you met and danced with there – well, by the time we got there after umpteen pints – were not really what you would have taken out proudly on your arm, although we certainly would have taken them to bed, given the chance. They wanted the former and we wanted the latter, sooner rather than later. But then the latter action would have gone for almost any young women of the time after a certain amount of alcohol.

There were those blokes I knew in the Air Force who swore that is was a waste of time going for good-looking girls; those types could afford to be choosy.

'The uglier they are, the more grateful and likely to do the business they are', was the theory of slightly older and suavely-challenged, not to mention cosmetically-deficient airmen I knew. One held the theory that in a chat-up situation, asking directly 'Do you fancy a fug?' or similar bold directness meant that for every ninety-nine who slapped your face, deeply offended, the one who said 'Yes, let's go', and then did, made it all worthwhile. I never tried it but I was assured it worked.

When there appeared to be a quantity of, let's say attractively-challenged females with few decent-looking ones abounding, at times if the ale was flowing well we would have a 'Grimmy contest', the aim was to win a competition to get off with the ugliest girl of the evening, to win a whip-round prize of a few pounds. It livened up many a quiet evening. Much healthy (or unhealthy) argument ensued at the bar during the contest, as to the points considered in such communal judging, extra points could be claimed for such aspects as excess weight and/or size, dermatologically-challenged visages and pizza-complexions, offensive odour, strange hairstyles or colour, any 'unusual' outstanding physical attributes. All such matters added spice to an argument before a vote was taken at the end of the evening, and the kitty awarded. On occasions, part of the prize also included telling the winner's partner of her award. I can't remember if it was true or not that one recipient of her award angrily rounded on her 'winner' to tell him that she also had participated in a similar contest with her friends – and he had won theirs!

Usually we hunted in pairs, in the ancient tradition. I had a few partners over the years but Steve and I worked best and most successfully together. We took in turns to 'go for the best one' but we knew each-others style well. While we were dancing or chatting to girls, we could feed off each other as to who was doing well and likely to succeed, indeed who wanted to was important. I'm sure the girls were doing the same but we had more success as we got better at it.

In my heyday, around 1970–71, I was actually going out with four young women at the same time, in various stages of passion. But there was one major downside that gave me problems at the time – all their names began with 'J' – Jo, Jill, Jean and Jan all featured large in my legend and I didn't half drop some clangers, especially after a few beers! Most of the time I flannelled my way through it if I got their names wrong but on one occasion I was in the crowded crew room in the late afternoon when the phone rang. I had just come on night shift at half-past four, having had a lovely leisurely day with my latest girlfriend Jan at her parents' house on nearby Hayling Island. The parents both worked during the day, so we had a very loving day in and out of bed and I was feeling very pleased and smugly contented with life.

A mate handed me the phone and winked, saying 'Call for you Mac – a young lady'. I took the phone and a female voice said, 'Hello, John...it's me. How are you?' in a sexy voice.

(erm, yes I'm ok, but er... who are you?)

Of course I daren't say that, trying desperately to listen for clues as to the owner of the voice, but she kept asking if I was alright, sounding unsure. Surely it wasn't my bed-mate from earlier on? Why would she ring so soon? Jean, my 'now-and-againer' midwife, a lovely woman I really messed about, wouldn't phone me at work – would she? She never had before, so that left Jo, who was away up in London with her parents as she was on holiday from college or Jill, the naughty telephonist, who I hadn't seen for a week or so (a floundering relationship, not going well) but who I owed a call.

I protested that it was very noisy in the crewroom and I could hardly hear. In truth, I could hear perfectly but just could not place who I was speaking to. In the end, unconvincingly and stalling for time, I promised to ring 'whoever' in a day or so when I finished nights but my mystery caller sounded very unconvinced.

Two days letter I received a letter from Jo, safely tucked away in London but very concerned at my phone performance and questioning our relationship. I was then able to piece together what happened and take the necessary action to reassure her by phoning her at her parents' house, when I was able to sound convincing enough, blaming the crewroom noise and my mates extracting the uric acid (that bit was true). Fortunately, she believed me!

But all good things must come to an end and as things were getting serious with Jan, I began to tone down my multiple fun. It was fun while it lasted but it was also too heavy, passionate, difficult, expensive and fraught with danger. You have to have a good memory and a lot of energy to carry on like that for long and while I enjoyed it immensely and it left me with many happy and funny memories, I wasn't sobbing myself to sleep when I began to go steady. Eventually, it became the beginning of the end for me as a single man.

But all that didn't happen until after I left the RAF. I still had a way to go in the fidelity stakes. I was too busy enjoying myself to stop altogether. Plus, I kept 'bumping into' Jean – sometimes accidently and sometimes deliberately. It seemed churlish not to take advantage of the situation!

There is no doubt that chasing young women played a huge part in my life during the five years I spent in the service of Her Majesty. Perhaps if I'd been a little less butterfly-like in my endeavours, I might have had more meaningful, deeper relationships, perhaps even becoming a nicer person in the process, dare I say. But is it the thrill of the chase that drives you on, not wanting to miss what is on offer, grabbing life with both hands (steady, John)? I don't know the answer. All I know is that I had a ball. Thanks girls, I wouldn't have missed it for the world – so there!

12.   The Demise of The Pig

My first car was terrific, a 1955 Austin A30. My Dad had taught me to drive in his big, well-maintained company car prior to entering the RAF in 1966 but I had failed my test and only had a provisional licence. On my trade training course at RAF Cosford I saw the Pig (registration number PYG 640) advertised for sale at £35. I got in for a test drive and concluded that it had no brakes, because when you put your foot on the pedal, only a very slight slowing motion ensued, bringing you gently to a stop about fifty yards away. I found out that this was normal in an old car, not like Dad's, and contracted to buy the Pig in several weeks' time when I had the full £35.

Unfortunately for me, an older RAF electrician doing a senior course to mine nipped in and bought it, much to my disgust, as he had the ready money. I watched him out on the car park, fitting ammeters and temperature gauges to it, like you do if you're a whiz-kid sparky (which I'm not). Imagine my delight when he sidled up to me a few days later to tell me that due to his endorsements his insurance quote was too high and he would have to wait some considerable time to re-apply at a lower cost, so... would I still like to buy it? I explained I still hadn't saved the £35 but as he was posted away the following week and he needed the money I offered him £30. I still had to borrow £5, but the Pig was now mine, cheaper and now with two instruments fitted – bargain!

I took the car down to the South Coast after I was posted there on completing training. I quickly passed my test and became quite popular, as there were more lads without cars than with them. But there was one problem. Although the Pig was a good runner when warmed up, she was a little bugger to start and got slowly worse with time. I was, and still am, absolutely useless with cars and several of my good mates with car know-how worked on this aspect of The Pig (amongst other tasks) but with little success.

To counter this problem, especially on an important Saturday night out, I would look for car-less lads getting ready to go out, the ones who I knew would be catching the bus off the camp. Pretending to casually notice they were also going out, I would offer them a lift, only for them to find themselves pushing The Pig twice round the car park before my pride and joy would condescend to stutter into life. I claimed 'that was unusual, she normally starts easily' and mostly got away with it, at least for a few more pushes. All was normally forgotten by the time I dropped them off without them having to pay the bus fare. Some even contributed to my petrol!

I think I had a couple of years of motoring before I received the grave news that the Pig had passed its last MOT; it was hopelessly rusty underneath. My sister and her husband had, for a while, been inviting me to go and see them in Swansea, where she was at college, some five-ish hours away by car. The Pig had a couple of months of legal life left, with MOT, tax and insurance running out then, when I set off for Swansea one weekend. A good friend, knowing my predicament in starting The Pig, had lent me his heavy-duty battery while his own car was off the road, to give The Pig a decent go at starting before it flattened the normal battery, so well-armed, off I went.

All seemed ok until, as I approached Wales's latest toy, the newly-opened Severn Bridge, a sort of ticking started to come from under the bonnet. The noise grew steadily louder as I passed Cardiff and by the time I reached Swansea the noise and reduced performance was embarrassing. It seemed Swansea was on the edge of a mountain, every street was either seriously up or down a horrendous incline and by the time I had found their house the noise was deafening. My brother-in-law came out, smiled and raised his eyebrows.

'Big-end gone, John?' he asked.

When I said I didn't know, he said he thought it sounded like that – and he was right. The next day we confirmed it over an inspection pit at their college, so in a terribly dangerous towing operation involving their washing line – it broke repeatedly – we set out for the local scrapyard. It was never going to be good news when the hulking great, sour South Whalian git who owned the yard offered me £8. He muttered that two tyres and the battery were ok, he could sell them on. Just in time, I remembered the battery wasn't mine and told Pitprop man it wasn't for sale.

'£6 then, boyo,' he growled – and that was that. Bye-bye to my beloved Pig!

On the Monday morning, after a great weekend, the demise of The Pig apart, they took me to the bus station with my small suitcase and (very) heavy-duty battery. The coach took me to Portsmouth and I persuaded the driver to drop me near the railway station, where I had to travel by rail two stops along to the village adjacent to our camp. The only way I could carry my cumbersome load was to hold the suitcase out in front of me, like an ice-cream girl at the cinema, with the battery sitting on top.

With some difficulty, I boarded the public bus from the train to complete my journey, using this embarrassing and awkward method. On alighting from the bus, I trudged across the parade square, which doubled as a car park, past all my mates' cars, into the block I lived in and staggered up the stairs to the first floor and the communal room I shared with a dozen others. The kind mate who had leant me the battery was lying on his bed and, on seeing my plight, leapt to his feet to grab his battery from me, offering the helpful words, 'Oh, Mac, you didn't have to bring the battery straight back, tomorrow would have done.'

'This is all that's left of my fuggin' car,' I gasped, before collapsing on my bed.

The Pig was dead, long live the Triumph Herald – but that's another story.

13.   Shiny Stories – Deeps Guard

'Erm... I was wondering – would it be possible to see the planes? I just wanted to show the kids.' Four sets of pleading eyes gazed out from inside the car. Well, they looked ok. I was bored senseless, so why not? I tried to look stern and military in my best uniform.

'Well, let's put it this way. If you tell me you're visiting the church, sign my permission book to that effect, drive very slowly straight down this road and across the airfield, you can see the planes from quite nearby. Please do not stop, do not take pictures or do anything stupid, or we'll both be in trouble. When you see the little car park by the private sailing club, opposite the church, park, get out, stretch your legs and look in the church if you want to, it's quite pretty. Then come back exactly the same way and I'll sign you out – does that sound ok?' That was my spiel, with permission one could visit the church, so I gave a few families a nice afternoon out while I was on 'Deeps Guard' duty.

This tedious guard duty came about once a year, usually on a Saturday or Sunday when our friends (not) the RAF police were given a rest. The road up to the camp was notoriously windy and unwelcoming and a sign saying *Ministry Of Defence Property – Keep Out* deterred most, but some would still approach the lowered barrier and usually ask to see the planes. Technically, as it was private property, we could refuse but if they asked nicely... well, why not? It gave me a kick when they thanked me and waved, all looking happy having seen the huge Hercules aircraft close up.

A big laugh one year was when a squadron of Air Training Corps cadets from Liverpool arrived for two weeks. The ATC were an occupational hazard to us permanent residents and we regarded them as a nuisance more than anything. On Deeps Guard that weekend was one 'Geordie' Harrison, a married man of some mean reputation, who lived in married quarters about fifteen miles from our base. He had come to stay for the weekend, arriving on Saturday and coming out with us on Saturday evening to have a good booze-up with the lads before returning home late Sunday after the guard.

Geordie's reputation was legendary. He was only about 5ft 5 but a very nasty piece of work when riled. Slightly built, with a wild cast in one eye, he always looked like he needed a shave, though no-one had the balls to tell him. Usually, he reserved his aggression for the football field, where he was regularly booked and sent off against the Navy, who he hated, but his temper was respected by those who knew him, as he was capable of exploding violently without much provocation.

So it came to pass that on the last bus back onto the camp on Saturday night, after the pubs had shut, a crowd of the young Scousers were making a bit of noise – like youngsters do – and Geordie told 'em to shut up. Apparently, they didn't like that and told Geordie to fug off – and more! If you didn't know Geordie – and they didn't – he didn't look much, quite puny really. But... well, I wasn't there but I know a couple of blokes who were and they said it was like a scene from a Wild West saloon, although it was all over in a flash. Two of them got up but went down even quicker as Geordie hit one in the face, nutted the second, kicked the first in the Max Wall's before kicking the second again, where it hurts of course. It was just before the stop outside the main gates. Geordie got off and melted away into the night as the Scousers dragged their wounded back to their block.

Naturally, the story spread around us the next morning like wildfire. The Liverpudlians were not popular with us, we didn't really like having the ATC around at the best of times, but this lot were lippy, cheeky little sods.

Most of us slept in on Sunday mornings after late-night Saturdays but Sunday lunch in the mess started at twelve, most of us hungry by then and an early lunch was usually the plan. I was with two or three others as we approached the mess, and to our surprise there was a small bunch of Scousers standing outside the main door with an RAF policeman. As we approached, they gave us the once-over but shook their heads to the copper. Two of them, big buggers as well, looked as if they had been in a bad car accident, black eyes, cuts and bruises, etc – and that was only their faces. I bet their balls were sore!

Of course, we all knew by then what had happened, who had done it and who they were looking for, but best of all – where he was! The culprit was sitting in a small brick-built sentry box affair half-a-mile down the road with his beret pulled so far down over his eyes it was hard to discern any features. On that duty it was possible to hide if you wanted to. Any approaching vehicle could be spotted from a distance. If the light blue special pass disc could be seen, you lifted the barrier and if anyone else came, a very cursory shake of the head and a quick point at the explanatory sign meant you didn't have to talk to anyone if you didn't want to.

Geordie didn't that day. We had tipped him off and took his meals down to him; as soon as six o'clock arrived, he was off camp like a shot, back to the safety of married quarters, miles away.

For the rest of the week he stayed with us, Up The Line, in our isolated, insulated private little world, and waited till the heat died down!

14. Justin

Shortly after my first posting to a real RAF station, I was in the mess having lunch when a vision walked past my table carrying his tray. I stared, astounded, because I had simply never seen anything quite like it in my service life before. It was Justin's hair that was the most startling aspect, it was simply the longest and most stylish I had ever seen on a British serviceman. In looks, I would liken him to Donovan, the UK's sixties answer to Bob Dylan. Justin's eyes were dark, with long black eyelashes; a straggly moustache half hid his mouth, running down either side of his lips to his chin. With his gypsyish mop of black curly hair falling carelessly over his forehead, ears and collar, with sallow, olive-coloured skin in truth he looked more like a pop singer in uniform, a la George Harrison in his Sergeant Pepper phase.

Our eyes met briefly, he shot me a defiant what-the-fug-are-you-looking-at, as if he was regularly contemptuous of such barely-concealed fascination. He went off to sit as far away as possible in a quiet corner alone to eat; that was nothing unusual with Justin, as I was to find out. He was hugely secretive and went to great lengths to guard his privacy. His name, I soon found out, was Justin Samuel Richwood-Broadman; he always insisted that was his real name, in the few times anyone dared to press him on the subject.

Within a few months of being posted to this new working RAF station, I was moved 'Up The Line' – i.e. onto the airfield itself, where our base was a wooden 'H' type building and I would be actually working on the aircraft themselves, on a weekly rotating shift pattern. This new way of life contrasted sharply with the previous one, which was in a boring wireless servicing bay every day, usually repairing small radio modules. This new shiftwork was a totally different regime to anything I had been used to before, very laid-back and seemingly discipline-free – and the working hours were markedly different.

I was told to report to a Sergeant Hughes one Monday morning, and I found him in a small room containing four other airman of various ranks below Sergeant, including... Justin! In a deep voice the diminutive Sergeant Hughes introduced himself as 'John', told me the others first names, and asked me what I liked to be called.

'Mac', I replied, disbelieving that everyone was on first name terms, with no acknowledgment of rank, but I loved it and took to it like a duck to water. This was where Justin worked and, as I was an adjacent trade to him, I began to get to know him better – very slowly, though, he kept himself very much to himself. I was living in the same billet (a block of six large rooms on three floors) as Justin, although in a different room. Soon, however, a coveted corner 'bedspace' became available directly opposite this mystical figure and I grabbed it quickly and moved in. Like everyone else, I was fascinated by Justin, the way he conducted himself and the way he adorned his personal bedspace.

We lived in a regulation long, narrow room with seventeen beds in it, nine down one side, eight the other, with a bricked-off room known as a 'bunk' to complement the space left. A corporal lived in the bunk, who was supposed to be in charge of the room, although no-one really took any notice, discipline was conveniently lax. Standard minimum government issue allowed one large locker (a single wardrobe, six feet high, two feet six inches wide) and one smaller bedside locker, not much really to keep all your worldly goods in, in that day and age. In actual fact, there were a considerable number of spare beds and lockers available – the camp was not full – so we were able to acquire and align spare large lockers round our beds, arranged to give us maximum privacy. By and large, considering we were members of Her Majesty's Services, we were treated like grown-ups, not young trainees, and were given adequate privacy, given what I considered the Second World War type of accommodation in 1967.

The hugely secretive Justin had taken this to extremes in his corner with two lines of 6ft high lockers at right angles forming two walls to complement his two permanent corner ones, which gave him virtually his own room. Only a narrow gap was left for access, which he curtained off. He actually had an Indian shawl affair covering this access to add to the overall dramatic effect. As I was now sharing a communal wall of tall lockers with Justin, and we worked together, we now became slightly more easy with each other but he could be very private and difficult if he wanted to be. We worked on the same shift and our trades were similar (I was radio and he was radar), so we saw a lot of each other. We even did a part-time job together (see the chapter on cleaning windows) but he was still a really private person. Most service people tend to be quite affable and rounded, especially when you share rooms and communal washing facilities, etc, but the reclusive Justin kept himself to himself very much and did not mix outside work, having civilian friends off-camp that you never saw.

The most fascinating things about Justin were his tastes in music, hair, clothes and artistic abilities. He never invited you into his bedspace, so to go in and have a butcher's you had to be doubly sure he had gone out before entering the hallowed area. He'd have gone mad if he'd caught you. Going in was like stepping into another world, belonging to a talented exponent of trendy taste, like a Carnaby Street boutique. The way he had made it meant there were no windows, so the light was deliberately dim, but every possible space on the walls was taken up with pictures, bizarre record covers and brightly coloured fabrics of reds, greens, yellows and purples. The *pièce de résistance* was a giant collage of heads that he had cut out and pasted together on a huge sheet of card, inspirationally derived no doubt from the famous Sergeant Pepper album cover. This massive work completely dominated one wall, making you feel uncomfortable, as if there were many eyes looking at you as you uninvitedly snooped round his weird habitat.

Justin was not averse to burning joss sticks and this heady, sickly incense was ever present, no doubt soaked into the fabrics that were creatively pinned and draped around the place. All in all, the whole effect was one of wondrous curiosity, as if you had stumbled accidentally into an eccentric designer's private world – hard to believe considering my own bedspace and 'normality 'was only a few feet away, my pin-ups, photos and a few personal items looking decidedly ordinary in comparison to Justin's psychedelic lair.

Once he was out of uniform, Justin's dress sense was extraordinary. His colours were purple, very fashionable in the flower power days of that year, pinks, mauves, blacks, with flowing styles, flared and loose a la Jimi Hendrix, as if he were an extravagant artist or pop star. But he craved not attracting attention on the camp, just the opposite, slinking out suddenly from his bedspace in arresting appearance, to go out who-knows-where into the dark night, as if he loathed daylight.

From the stores, Justin somehow managed to acquire another RAF greatcoat, no main achievement in those days. It wasn't known how he persuaded them that he had lost his, had it stolen or whatever, but he pulled it off it, and had the other one altered considerably to look fantastic in it when he went out. He removed the regulation epaulettes, had it dyed navy blue and replaced the brass buttons with big trendy dark blue ones. That style was all the rage in those late-sixties fashion-conscious days, and Justin caught the mood perfectly.

Musically Justin was an enigma to me: his tastes were very varied and out-of-time with his contemporaries, who embraced the rock and roll era of Elvis, Buddy Holly and early Cliff Richard. He knew what he liked and was scathing and contemptuous about what he didn't, and there was little room in between. He was about eight or nine years older than me, indeed as I was only eighteen almost everyone seemed older at first. My preferred musical tastes included Tamla Motown, The Beach Boys and modern late sixties stuff which my elder workmates despised loudly. But Justin introduced me to Reggae, Prince Buster, Bob Marley ... and Leonard Cohen! Hating the latter at first, I grew to love him, and still do today. I try to sing some of his songs today on my guitar, in my opinion he is something else, but of course most people, then and now, dismiss his songs as just *music to slash your wrists by*.

Justin seemed to take no real interest in women as we others did, with our pictures of nude women adorning our bedspaces and sex being an ever-present popular subject of discussion. But about a year after I had first met him Justin did start going out steadily with a girl from a nearby village, in typical secretive Justin style. No-one had ever seen or heard of her before and we didn't know her name. In truth, when she did briefly emerge, she was a female version of him: dark, curly hair, slim, trendily dressed and the last I heard of him he was engaged to her.

Justin was still there when I left the RAF in 1972, exactly the same as when I first saw him four years previously: mean, mysterious, moody, morose and yet magnificent. I never heard him shout (he could swear all right), move quickly or threaten anyone. But everyone, including his superiors, gave him room and respect. He seemed to engender that quality in people. He was never in trouble or caused any, he just got on with the job quietly as requested.

I often wonder what became of the most unlikely-looking and acting serviceman I ever came across.

15. Jo Haynes

I think her full name was Josephine, another of the 'J' brigade. I had developed an unfortunate streak of going out with a number of girls whose Christian names began with 'J' and I got it wrong on a number of occasions: especially when I'd had a few and stumbled over their name. I think, although it wasn't cool to admit it, that I met Jo on a blind date (not usually done unless desperate), through a ginger RAF bloke I knew and his girlfriend, and Jo was one of her friends. 'Ging' was not one of my mates who I knocked about with, he was fairly straight regarding booze and birds, which of course I wasn't. What I mean by that was that in our group we drank regularly to excess, a drink was six pints, and going for a night out meant an average of twelve to fourteen pints, which was par for the course. That would have killed Ging, three pints was too much!

In those days young women were very much on the '4F' formula, i.e. Find 'em, Feel 'em, Fug 'em and Forget 'em. Long term relationships were not on our agenda, not for our crowd, but as I said, Ging was not one of us, he went out with his girlfriend – steadily – nicely – truthfully. In actual fact, I did go out with Jo for about six months, much longer than my normal romances. Why was that? Well, for a start, she was very attractive (my mate Steve really fancied her – well her lovely generously shaped breasts and long blonde hair, anyway). She was quite tall, about five feet seven (I usually went out with smaller girls) slimmish, well-turned out with shoulder-length blonde hair. Her face was almost nun-like, pale and innocent in manner, quiet and reserved. I suppose the blind-date bit got round the fact that if I had seen her in a disco or one of our usual pick-up places, I would not have gone for her type – although she was very pretty, very attractive to have on your arm, good for the ego.

For something to do to keep my brain active, I took a couple of 'O' levels while in the RAF, one being history. Jo either had been, or was studying history, and helped me with my studies, lending me some books. She wanted to be a teacher and had a lovely gentle way of imparting knowledge to you without being patronising. Jo was a student at a teachers' training college near Bognor and had digs in a big house off the seafront with two or three others girls, staying with a nice family who looked after them all. We had not been going out long, but were getting on well and had taken to kissing and cuddling – and a bit more – in the front seat of my old bench-seated Vauxhall Victor (column gear change, convenient for romance), parking quietly down the road from her digs before she went in. One night we were getting a bit carried away, I got bold and asked her, straight out, but in a gentle way, if she would perform an orally-specific sex act on me, as we were nearly there at the time – or so it seemed to me.

She didn't reply straightaway but didn't slap my face or refuse point-blank either at the suggestion, as might have been in those not-as-sexually-permissive-as-you-might-think days. As there was a silence, I apologised, murmuring that it was ok if she didn't want to but, to my amazement, she said softly, 'Yes, I'll do it – you'll be cross if I don't'. Of all the responses I thought I might get, I didn't expect that one – did that mean – all I had to do was get cross to... before I could examine this fascinating possibility further, her lovely blonde head slid downwards and she did it to me anyway, to my amazement and incredulous delight. As the saying goes – if you don't ask, you don't get – I learnt a lot that night.

As things were now moving in the right direction (downwards?), I worked out an evil plan for the full Monty. I always walked her back to her house, in via the discreet back gate and up to the girls own door at the back of the house, which I found out led privately straight up to the girls bedrooms. Outside we always kissed good night tenderly, and parted, calling good night as I walked back to the gate. My devious plan, which I put to Jo, was that she would go in, but leave the back door slightly open, I would head down the path, calling goodnight, rattle the gate, but then quickly and quietly double back and slip inside the door, before closing it as silently as possible. Aren't young women surprising and wonderful? Because, to my amazement, she went through the plan again with me calmly, nodding her head, then squeezing my hand she said,

'Ok, John: when shall we do it?' My bluff soundly called, with heart beating like a drum and trying to appear cool (which I wasn't), I casually suggested 'Erm... Sunday?'

'Yes, that's a good night', my lovely fellow-conspirator agreed. 'They go to bed early on Sunday nights to get up for work in good time on Mondays'. A thought flashed through my mind – surely she hadn't done this before? I thought about it (once), conveniently dismissed the idea, put it down to my aftershave and looked forward to the weekend like no other. And that is exactly what happened the following Sunday night. It went like clockwork, Jo and I consummating our relationship in her little single bed that night. After everyone had gone off to work and college that day, claiming sickness, Jo stayed with me. Much later in the morning I sneaked out of the back door and away. I thought all my birthdays had come at once, so to speak!

The only problem was, cad-like, I did not want a steady relationship leading to the 'M' word, which Ging and his girl were contemplating. There were some other nights in Jo's bed and in a few different places, including my car and the beach. One night we stayed the night at a party, sleeping and loving on the settee downstairs when everyone had gone. When Steve came to wake us in the morning we were both naked except for a blanket and he made sure he got a good look at what was a delightful sight (Jo, not me) and often referred to her boobs in glowing terms afterwards. Well, I have to admit they were a bit special; she looked sensational naked.

Jo features elsewhere in this book, once when we gave her a lift home one weekend en route to a mate's wedding and another time when she embarrassingly phoned me at work and I didn't know who it was (I thought she was someone else). We parted a little abruptly eventually. I think we had had words, as we weren't seeing enough of each other as far as she was concerned and a parting of the ways ensued. Afterwards she wrote me a letter, tersely asking for her history books she had lent me to be returned and, from the letter I quote: 'especially after the very shabby way in which you treated me'. Needless to say, I showed it (discreetly, I thought) to one of the lads. It caused great amusement as he then paraded the letter round our circle with great glee. It disappeared and I eventually found it pinned to the noticeboard, adorned with ribald comments, and for a while I had to endure comments like 'Hey, here comes Shabby!' or confidentially (loudly) whispered 'Aren't you the bloke who treats women shabbily?'

Jo really was a lovely modern girl of the sixties, very 'Marianne Faithful' in her looks and dress and I should have treated her better. I often wonder what happened to the lovely Jo.

My loss, wasn't it?

16.   Andy, Blind Dates and Cornish Pastis (sic)

I haven't to date mentioned my mate from school, Andy. This is largely because these stories are from a period during which our friendship was rather strained, mainly due to the fact that we were both changing and moving on, going our separate ways in ever-widening directions. Andy and I lived on the next road to each other in Nottingham, went to the same primary and grammar schools together, joined the Air Training Corps together, found girls and two-wheeled motor transport heaven together; but there were also many differences.

Andy was clever. I wasn't. He never did any revision and easily passed eight 'O' levels. Matters were made worse because I was on holiday with him and his family in Anglesey when the results came out. It seemed the end of the world when I only passed three and my father, God bless him, told me he expected me to 'go down the pit' (we lived in a mining area), which was not what was expected of me. I apologise straight away to all brave and honest miners, no disrespect intended, but that's the way it was in those days.

My career path from there is mentioned elsewhere, but I became a Mod, going up the scooter route, whereas Andy was a motorbike man, although he was never a greaser or a rocker. One of the few times I got one over on him in those days was when we took our tests on the same day. I passed and he failed, much to his disgust. We had just discovered girls at the same time and we were going out with two friends who both obviously wanted us to pass so that they could ride legally on the back. Tony re-took his test and passed a few months later, ironically on my scooter, as his bike was off the road. My beloved Lambretta was known affectionately known as *Bubbles*. I still have an old Vespa today *Bubbles 2* – I just love scooters, always have.

It seemed nothing could stop Andy in those days on his path to success. I eventually joined the Royal Air Force but Andy, via the

ATC. obtained a Flying Scholarship, giving him an unheard of private pilot's licence at the age of seventeen. Although the Air Force were courting him, Andy's ambitions were to be an airline pilot for BEA or BOAC. It seemed to me that nothing could get in his way. But it did.

When I joined up I made a point of sending him a postcard from almost everywhere I travelled to, particularly anywhere exotic, obviously intended to piss him off. It worked a treat, he told me later how digging himself out of bed on a cold morning and dragging himself to school or college on a bitterly cold, grey winter's day, it really got him going when he received a postcard from Bermuda or Singapore, telling him what a great time I was having.

Disaster struck for poor Andy on two fronts while I was away having fun in the RAF. By this time, he had graduated to cars and hurtled round everywhere in an old Ford Popular, his pride and joy. His trademark was driving too fast with his window always down, his right elbow resting on the sill. One day he went round a left turn too sharply, the car turned over and Andy trapped his arm underneath. The upshot was that he severely damaged his arm above and below his elbow, which was also dislocated and, up until the time we lost contact in the mid 1970's, he still had not regained full use of his arm. Unfortunately that meant he could not pass a medical necessary for him to keep flying, which made him very bitter.

I don't know what was going on in Andy's head at the time but to compound this accident he somehow managed to fail two of his three 'A' levels and it seemed the bottom dropped out of his world. The next time I came home for a visit, he had left school and was studying metallurgy at a college in Derby, backed by Rolls Royce. I think, but am not sure, that that is what he eventually became, a metallurgist. By the time I went to his wedding in Lancashire, in about 1974, now aged twenty-five, I think he was a much-changed man, very serious and far from the happy, loud, confident, funny youth I grew up with.

Over my five years in the RAF I came home to Nottingham about every six months, I would guess, although there was never really any regular plan. I would alert Andy of when I was coming and sometimes he would arrange a blind date for me with the friend of the girl he was currently dating. Unlike me, in those days he tended to go out with the same girl for months on end and one in particular of his girlfriends, Maggie, took a shine to me. I think it was because she saw me as fun, with my different stories of forces life, in direct comparison to the serious young man Andy was turning into. I had a twenty-first birthday party at a church hall in Nottingham and, as I was unattached at the time, Maggie insisted on dancing with me all evening, much to everyone's amusement and Andy's disgust (he hated dancing), so I obliged, but in the slowies I could feel his eyes boring into my back as Maggie snuggled up close.

One weekend when I was home he was going out with a girl called Sue from teacher's training college. Andy said there was a disco at the college on the Saturday and would I like to meet his girl's friend that evening? I said ok and we went in his car; the college was miles out in the country. My 'date' – if you can call it that – was a complete disaster. We had nothing in common, she was a seriously-minded out-and-out academic with delusions of grandeur and I was a young serviceman home on leave, up for a laugh and a joke. I could find no middle ground with this one, despite trying hard. At one time it go so bad she went off to talk to her college friends, male and female, a cliquey lot who didn't mix, leaving me to play gooseberry to Andy and Sue. No problem really, but a snag developed as the evening drew to a close. Andy's highlight of the week, he privately explained, was a sexually explicit encounter with his love, which usually took place late on a Saturday evening in her room before outsiders had to leave. This night was no exception, and he intended to keep up normal service, but I was the problem.

He had made certain contingency plans, which unfortunately were not looking good, due to 'Preppy' and I not hitting it off. Despite my protestations that I would wait in the cold car, to my surprise Preppy returned towards the end of the disco, half-heartedly apologised for her absence and offered me a coffee in her room. As it was in earshot of the other two and the slightly 'duty-bound' way she said it, made me almost sure she had not come to her senses and realised that she was missing a golden opportunity for a fantastic roll in the hay while the others did likewise. It was to be purely business – suited me!

I followed her back to her small room, very Spartan and office-like, certainly no pictures on the wall of pop stars or film heart-throbs of the day. I sat down on the only chair and tried once again to make small talk, to see if there was any common ground. There wasn't. I fell silent and she tried, but it was on an academic subject of which I had no knowledge. In desperation, she talked about a holiday in rural France she had had recently, where I had never been. The situation began to feel like commoner and aristocrat, Princess and pauper, and so after another uncomfortable silence (I was beginning to wonder how long it took Andy and Sue to do it), to my complete surprise she suddenly blurted out,

'Do you like Pastis?' I was completely taken aback, looking round the small, basic room. Nowhere could I see any mini-oven, anything that could heat a pie, but I have always had a taste for savoury items and well... it was quite late, I'd had a few beers and was always hungry at that time of night.

'Cornish?' I piped up helpfully, looking around for the secret supply. If one word destroyed our relationship forever, it was that. She blanched visibly, winced and said, very firmly and deliberately, as if explaining to a child.

'It's ... a ... French ... ap-er-it-ive.'

At the time I did not see the humour in this and neither did she, as I declined her generous offer. That effectively killed the conversation stone-dead and sealed our condemned relationship forever. We waited quietly until we got the call, which seemed hours when you're in the company of someone you don't want to be with. At least Andy was happy on the way home as he described his girlfriend's athleticism in bed.

For my part, when I arrived safely back in my more common world of fellow coarse servicemen, I related the story to my mates, who all roared at my peasant upbringing being so cruelly exposed. One in particular, a blunt Yorkshireman called Graham, loved the story and often on nights when we were boozing and the conversation lulled, he would get me to repeat it.

'Owz it go?' he would ask. 'She said – do you like Cornish? And you said – what – pasties?'

I would repeat it until he got it, by which time he was paralytic with laughter. I could just imagine him repeating it back in Yorkshire with his heavy accent, getting it wrong, to puzzled looks.

Andy later married a strongly-spoken, no-shades-of grey Lancashire girl and he invited all my family. It was a fairly serious teetotal affair, my father was horrified there was no booze at the reception and he ordered a bottle of wine to the undisguised disgust of those around him. Later back at the bride's family home the atmosphere was still deadly dull, all of us crammed into one room sipping tea, until my Mum's and Andy's brother's wife, the lovely Isabel's eyes met from opposite sides of the room. Uncle Sam had protested mildly, but in truth was secretly delighted to be asked to play the organ in the corner, and had just started when Isabel raised her eyes to heaven in a desperate plea, noted by Mum who started to giggle.

That started Isabel off, cues for glares and tuts from Sam's fan club. It was one of those situations where if you see the funny side of it... Mum looked at me, and I was done for, tears began to roll down Isabel's cheeks as she tried to suppress her laughter, but Sam played on, oblivious to his divided audience.

That was really the finish of Andy and I. We soon lost touch after his wedding although to me it was no great loss. We had had some good fun as lads but were never really close as mates, as we were two very different characters, and he had changed so much in the latter years of our friendship.

Such is life!

Basic Training, February 1967.

First home leave, March 1967.

Mac and his Pig, RAF Cosford, May 1967.

Dave's van, en route to The Cider House, Staffordshire, June 1967.

Gan, Maldives 1968.

Gordon's wedding, Norfolk 1969.

Thorney Island Sunday team, 1970. Mac, back row, third from left.

Camping holiday in Cornwall, August 1968.

That Hercules, Larges, Azores, June 1971.

SAC in Herc

Dave and Mac, Bermuda beach, December 1970.

Empire State Building, New York, 1971 – impressive view!

RAF Thorney Island –The Mess we 'cracked'.

Outside Thorney Island Sailing Club 2009.

The block where I lived for 4½ years.

The Author 2010.

17. Bradley

Brian Bradley was the original gentle giant, a big, amiable, lumbering hulk of a man, always in trouble, always seemingly through no fault of his own. 'Bradley' as he was known, sometimes disparagingly, was easily led. He was always the fall guy, the one who got caught, while the smaller, nimbler ones like me got away with it. One night we went to a nightclub, three or four of us, in his car, I believe. When we arrived it was absolutely sheeting down with rain and we had to park miles away. A suggestion was made to cut across the gardens to avoid getting completely soaked, which we all agreed would be best.

I was last and Bradley was running just ahead of me. I am not normally malicious or devious but some devilment – or a few pints – got into me that night as I thought it would be fun to clip my giant mate's ankles together for a laugh. But it went much worse than I intended. Instead of slipping on the wet grass, Bradley managed to stagger several yards further before crashing full length into a flowerbed full of roses. The horror of what I had done was revealed as he pulled himself up, covered in mud from head to foot, including his face, with scratches on his hands, the new chocolate-brown jacket he had just bought, which had looked very smart, now covered in mud. Most people would have grabbed me by the throat and punched me, I'm sure, but I told you he was gentle. He just stared at me disbelievingly, shaking his head as he asked, mystified, 'What did you do that for?'

I protested, probably unconvincingly, that I had slid on the wet grass myself, and inadvertently clipped his heel. Accidents had always dogged Brian Bradley's life, so he wearily trudged in the direction of the club, explaining his plight at the door, where they reluctantly let him into the gents. There we all tried, pretty unsuccessfully, to patch him up. I dared not admit to anyone that I did it deliberately. I think they believed me but in truth it was the sort of thing he did himself all the time!

In the 'block' where we all lived, there were between fourteen and seventeen of us living in the big, long room at any one time. Most of us were normalish height and build, the only other inhabitant of a similar size to Bradley was a fat giant called Anderson. He wasn't really one of us, working in another part of the camp, but he was ok, very disorganised and a bit scruffy in his normal dress and reasonably cheerful and happy with his lot. We all used to borrow each other's clothes at times, well, those that fitted anyway, usually when we wanted to impress a girl who we had taken out a few times, to make it look as though our wardrobe was more extensive than it actually was. It was usually done on a 'tit for tat' basis and in general the system worked. But, of course, only Anderson and Bradley were of such similar size that they could wear each other's but no-one else's clothes.

Early one Saturday evening we were all watching Paddy Whiteside's TV at one end of the room. In came Bradley, ironed himself a huge blue and white striped shirt the size of a tent, left it on a hanger and went for a bath, where he usually died for an hour or so. In came Anderson: ten minutes in the bathroom and back to get ready to go out. He rooted through his crumpled pile of clothes, sniffing distastefully at most before rejecting them. He finally looked across the room to where Bradley slept. As we nudged each other, nodding and sniggering, over he went and plucked the very smart clean pressed shirt from the hanger. Five minutes later Anderson was perfectly dressed and ready to go out, briefly pausing to cross once more to pluck Bradleys expensive 'Brut' aftershave out from its hiding place under his pillow (everyone knew it was there), and generously splashing it liberally over himself.

As he passed us on the way out, he bade us a cheery, 'See you lads tomorrow, I'm on a cert tonight.'

We waited expectantly and, after about half an hour, Bradley emerged, red and steaming, in a towel. He was so slow in everything he did, drying, powdering and finally putting his pants and socks on. We couldn't wait. He wandered over to his locker, the single wardrobe where he kept most of his clothes, and began leafing through them. Very gradually it began to dawn on him that something was not right, as he searched with greater purpose.

Eventually the penny began to drop and he turned and approached us with a puzzled look on his face.

'Has Anderson been in?' We tried to smother our laughter, pretending to laugh at the television.

'Erm, yes... I think so', said Paddy, almost with a straight face.

Bradley turned and went back for another search, his face slowly reddening as he realised what had happened.

'The bastard! He's taken my fuggin' clean shirt, the one I ironed to go out in!'

To cries of 'No!' 'Really?' 'The bastard!' we rolled about in laughter, as Bradley, now incredulous and open-mouthed, came to terms with his loss.

But, as usual with Bradley, his amiable nature quickly forgot it, he donned a slightly-used one and went off happily, not remembering it until days later – and by then he just laughed it off – with Anderson, of course!

18. Jean Bull

Jean was one of those girls – women, I should say, for she was very mature and several years older than me – who wouldn't stand out in a crowd but she was a very interesting and unusual person. If this sounds hugely conceited, it's not meant to be, but I suppose normally I wouldn't have looked at her twice. She was a little plain, a little *wouldn't say boo to a goose* but the circumstances we met under were unusual. There was a sort of unofficial party in the nurses' home one Saturday night and although I knew my way round there fairly well, for some reason this night I arrived late and on my own. When I entered the door it seemed the pretty ones had all gone, in fact most had, but then I spotted Jean, sitting quietly on her own.

She was short, just over five feet one, but not skinny. I was never a fan of skin and bone, never have been. I prefer my women curvy – there, I've said it! I have to admit I'd had a fair bit to drink that night and was in a devil-may-care mood. I stood cockily in the entrance to the large lounge being used for dancing and drinking. As our eyes met, I pointed at her and beckoned with my forefinger, very macho. She mouthed an innocent 'Who, me?' and I nodded authoritatively, mouthing back 'Yes, you'. She got up and crossed the room to greet me. I would add at this point, that type of caveman approach was not me at all. In reality I'm quite shy (honest) and couldn't and wouldn't have normally acted like that; but the drink helped...

We seemed to click straightaway, talking as if we had known each other for ages. She was very funny and – different. I think, but don't remember for sure, that we became lovers that night. If we didn't exactly then, it was certainly very intimate. In truth, I was going out with someone else at the time, who, I'm ashamed to say, I was more interested in, but Jean and I had a lovely easygoing relationship with each other from the start and in bed she was great fun, very natural and matter-of-fact about everything. I was full of the usual hang-ups that young men of that age have about their performance, size, endurance, etc – it all seems so amusing now looking back – if I only knew then what I know now...

Jean was a midwife. I never found out how old she actually was. She could have been ten years older than me. It was obvious to us both that I was quite a bit younger and I was immature in comparison to Jean. One evening she solemnly presented me with a pamphlet that the midwives gave to all pregnant and/or postnatal mothers concerning contraception, the various methods discussed with diagrams to explain, leaving little room for confusion. Perhaps – or in retrospect, definitely – Jean had noted my cavalier approach to such matters, arrogantly believing (at the time, I hasten to admit) it was the woman's responsibility in those supposedly permissive days to arrange contraception. Jean suggested I read the pamphlet, which I did voraciously. Dutifully I passed it round the lads for detailed perusal – it made for great mealtimes discussions in the mess -knowing that the information therein was much more detailed and thorough than any such verbal (and therefore theoretic) knowledge we held.

In a pub one night I returned it to her, thanking her earnestly for her thoughtfulness and how much valuable information I (and we) had learnt as a result. Jean looked deeply into my eyes, leaned over to me so our faces met, and said softly, 'Just remember, John. There is only one foolproof method of contraception.'

'The pill ?' She shook her head.

'The coil?' I tried to remember the alleged percentage success rates claimed. Jean shook her head gravely again, as she did with all my subsequent efforts.

'What is it then?' I asked eventually, puzzled. She leaned so close to me our lips brushed and we kissed lightly, sexily. She pulled back a fraction and said, firmly but saucily, her dark eyes sparkling, 'Abstinence, John – abstinence!'

That put me in my place – well, for half an hour or so, anyway!

One of the things I loved about Jean was her complete lack of inhibitions, so different to most young women I went out with at the time. One afternoon, after a liquid lunch, early on in our relationship we were lying on top of her bed in the nurses home and I was fumbling about trying to wrestle her skirt up and her knickers down at the same time, the two operations seemingly at odds when attempted horizontally. Quietly amused for a few minutes as she watched my inane efforts, she squeezed my hand, rolled gently to the edge of the bed and, getting off, coyly removed the offending garments (and everything else) before – seamlessly – perhaps not the right word? – re-joining me on the bed, completely naked, smiling gently as she wriggled closer, saying soothingly, 'There... is that better?'

In those days of endless pursuit of lithe young women, coupled with many rejections and unhelpful behaviour in such similar situations, this was definitely totally unexpected but very welcome. But then Jean was always thoughtful and, well, understanding and helpful towards me in my circumstances. I noted she always wore black underwear and when I queried it she gave me the unequivocal reply, 'It's good for morale!' Can't argue with that...

Months later, when I was seriously seeing a different young lady (another nurse) I woke up in bed with Jean without much idea how I got there. My car was parked fifty yards down the road from the other nurses home where my new love lived but Jean was wonderfully discreet, dare I say hugely understanding, of my errant behaviour. I'm ashamed to say today that I exploited our friendship, in that I would phone her or take her out when things were quiet, or I was a bit the worse for wear late at night and wanted company, and she was always there for me.

One night in the Sailing Club she was with someone else and when he went to the loo I beckoned her over, as I had done originally. She left her companion, came over to me, then, returning briefly to explain to him – whatever, I don't know – we left and spent the night together. Looking back, it's a wonder he didn't hit me, or at least say something.

It was with Jean that I went to see the hugely successful musical 'Hair' in Southsea on its UK tour. We both loved it for its boldness, fantastic music and dancing. Nudity wasn't in and definitely not done on the stage then, so when the final curtain came and all the members stripped off, everyone stood and cheered. It was a terrific show, very much of its time.

One of my mates, who shall remain nameless but is featured elsewhere, held a candle for Jean and was aware of how badly I treated her from an envious and disapproving position. As far as I remember, he later pursued her to Canada, where I believe she moved eventually.

She was a great sport, a lovely person who was always there for me, always supportive and available and I have a very soft spot in my heart for her.

Wherever she is today, I hope she is happy.

She deserves to be.

19. Did He Save Our Lives?

I am not really a superstitious person. I've tried it but when I forgot not to cross the spoons after using them, my testicles did not become square and fester in the corners. But hey, I don't knock it. If you don't like walking under ladders on Friday 13th, if a black cat crosses your path and you immediately defecate your rompers, so be it. Superstition just might have saved my life, as well as others.

We were returning from Bermuda on a NAVEX training exercise, for trainee aircrews to complete long-distance hauls. Aircraft ground crew like my mate Alec and I were enjoying a 'jolly', which meant we were taken along on the trip as a perk, only required to do basic aircraft handling work where and when expected. We had left cold old England in the early spring and flown in our C130 Hercules across the Atlantic to Bermuda, where we had spent a terrific night in a lovely hotel overlooking the bay. We then continued on our way to the Azores to spend a second night away, this time as guests of our American friends at the massive American Air Force base there called Larges. I need to add and emphasise at this point that in sharp contrast to we British, the Yanks really know how to treat their forces. Everything American was first-class and in comparison everything we had was strictly second-class – accommodation, food, uniforms, bullshit, you name it, in every department they outshone us.

The previous night we had been entertained as guests of the Americans at their swish nightclub on the base, where prominent American entertainers were known to appear. As visitors, we had to be signed into the club by the biggest, blackest security sergeant I have ever seen. He gazed gravely at each of us for a few seconds in turn before booming out, in a double-bass voice that came up from his bootlaces, 'Are y'all *just* men?' emphasising 'just' as a true virtue required by all visitors. We all vigorously nodded, assuring him that we were, and he welcomed us in as his guests. As a consequence of our warm welcome we had slight hangovers the next morning as we prepared the aircraft to take us back to the UK and home.

The quartermaster (today known more grandly as the loadmaster) was in charge of anything we were carrying, either the contents of the hold, if freight, and/or in charge of any passengers' safety and comfort – although there was not a lot of the latter on Hercules aircraft – plus any in-flight catering. He was not, in any way, in charge of anything technical, I stress, there was an flight engineer on board as part of the crew and almost everyone aboard our flight was more technically-minded than our quartermaster. But this one was a senior serviceman with many flying hours behind him and over the years had developed a slightly nervy habit of walking fully round every aircraft he was going to fly in, just once, immediately prior to each flight.

This particular trip, he started from the access door on the right as you look at the Hercules, just below and behind the cockpit, then walking back to the rear and rounding the back of the plane, to then walking up the starboard (right-hand) side of the aircraft. Our engines were beginning to run up as he passed the starboard wing when he stopped, puzzled at something he saw on the main fuselage, just forward of the wing. He went over to investigate. About ten feet up from the ground he noticed a thin line down the skin of the plane, about a foot long, running exactly top to bottom. The line was only visible clearly from the back, from where the quartermaster had noticed it. It was almost impossible to see full on at right angles and invisible from the front. We were all called in turn to have a look but it seemed a mystery to everyone as it was so high, so the engines were all shut down and a ladder brought out.

To everyone's shock, it was actually a crack in the metal skin of the plane and, to make matters worse, it was actually down a line of rivets. Personally I was astounded, when the soundproofing inside was stripped away to reveal the bare facts, which were that you could clearly see daylight from inside. I was also shocked to discover that the skin of the aircraft was about the thickness of a baked bean tin. Up to that point I had no idea it was so thin. But what had also given everyone a cold shiver was that unless the crack had appeared in the last eighteen hours or so since we had landed in the Azores – unlikely – then we must have flown like that from Bermuda, pressurized at about 30,000 feet. Scary, eh?

How long had it been there? Why hadn't we noticed it? Why no sound or pressure problems? And, of course, the 64,000 dollar question ... what we were going to do now?

In such situations, clarification is needed from above – and I don't mean God. Urgent signals began to flash their way around the world for all aircraft of the same type as ours to be checked for similar cracks. We heard afterwards that there were none. As ground crew we were used to such urgent checks, we were often sent to check similar items where another plane of the same type had developed a serious problem somewhere, and all planes needed to be checked before any further flights took place.

So, after nearly twenty-four tense hours, the signal came back from on high that it was a one-off and to 'get it fixed' at local level. Larges was on an island owned by the Portuguese and early the next morning a tanned little local man in overalls came to our aircraft on a tractor, pulling a small compressor behind him. He went up the by now well-trodden ladder and measured up, then produced a small piece of silver metal. This he trimmed expertly into a size of about eighteen inches long and four inches wide. He then neatly pock-riveted the new piece over the offending split. In those days the camouflage of the Hercules was made up of various shades of diarrhoea-brown, so, as you can imagine, the new piece shone brightly in the sun. No missing it now!

Then it had to be air tested by taking the plane on a short test flight, without us on board, fortunately. All seemed in order so, with our luggage and us all aboard this time, we took off and, after a quick circuit of the lovely tiny island, headed for home. Needless to say, we made it home in one piece, much to our relief. Soon afterwards, for some reason that escapes me, four of our planes were transferred to RAF Lyneham permanently, that aircraft one being one of them. The following year, I was down doing a stint on the visiting aircraft pan, where a visiting Hercules taxied in.

'Isn't that the kite (plane) you went to Bermuda in, the one with the crack?' observed an eagle-eyed colleague. On looking closer, it was. Of course, only I would know exactly where to look; anyone else would not have found it. Yes, the patch was still there, except that it had been cleverly sprayed over to blend in with the faeces-coloured rest of the fuselage and, in truth, you would not have been able to spot it if you didn't know about it– but I knew.

I was a bit disappointed. I expected the whole front of the aircraft would have been sawn off and replaced – bet the Yanks would have done! So, what was the truth? When had the crack occurred and how long before it was luckily discovered? I have no idea of the answers, all I know is that it was there for all to see and yet it was discovered by someone whose job it wasn't. All I will say is that I never knock superstition – it possibly saved my life!

20. 'Spanner' Harris

Spanner was one of the laziest sods I've ever met. Neither was he a particularly clean specimen: a bit spotty, throw in scruffy, could do with a hair wash and he was someone with not a lot going for him. About five feet seven, more-fat-on-a-chip, he would have to run around in the shower to get wet; that's if he ever went near running water (doubtful). Just to explain his name, it had nothing to do with him being a rigger (airframe technician) or for that matter anything technical. 'Spanner' was a nickname for someone not experienced with women but well-acquainted with his right hand, if you catch my meaning. If you don't, I'll spell it out – it was short for 'wanking spanner', meaning hand relief. Got it yet?

I never actually knew where Spanner called home, unlike most of us, and he never went home there, wherever it was. I suppose his accent and the fact he supported Chelsea meant he was a Londoner but he never talked about it and I don't recall anyone asking. I also never knew his Christian name; to everyone, including those in charge, he was just *Spanner*. He had a reputation for being first to the bar but last to put his hand in his pocket. There's always one, isn't there? Ours was Spanner. He was your complete pub entertainer, absolutely at home in one, with an impressive fund of jokes and stories. I liked and knew a few jokes and he and I used to play our own version of *Jokers Wild*, a TV game where someone gave you a subject and you had to tell a joke about it. With my memory for banal rubbish I wasn't bad at it and neither was he.

Most of us didn't smoke but it was Spanner's worst vice. On camp he and I always slept in separate rooms, we were never close mates, but on one detachment in Cyprus I had the misfortune to sleep in the next bed. The first morning, as light began to poke through the window shutters, I heard a strange noise. It sounded like a small caged animal trying frantically to scratch its way out of captivity and it took me a minute in my befuddled state to work out what it was. After a few seconds the panicky scratching on the top of the wooden locker (cabinet) that existed by every RAF bed stopped, to be replaced by a fumbling noise, then a click, one or two strikes and an igniting sound and finally a long, deep intake of breath, followed by an equally long satisfied exhalation. Spanner had found and lit his first cigarette of the day, probably before opening his eyes. His two most treasured possessions in life were twenty Number Six and a Zippo lighter.

He shared with all of us a love of football, although unfortunately supporting Chelsea, but no-one's perfect! He could, under duress, play the game too, but being bone idle he rarely ran or challenged for the ball. He spent most of the time redundant, way out on the right wing, his favoured position, and if you passed it too far in front of him, forget it. We used to scream at him, cajole him, goad him, swear at him and sometimes – rarely – he would deliver. He was capable, on occasions, of threading a perfect through ball for someone to run on to, or even getting to the by line now and again (rare) to deliver a cross, tailor-made for a striker who could head the ball. In the few instances when he did, we would not hear the last of it for weeks. Spanner could talk a game better than he played – and he could really talk when he got going.

Apart from football, he excelled in pub card games like crib, crash (an RAF card game) and brag. He also loved to play bridge. I didn't play but I could see he was good at it. I learnt the hard way just how good he was and I am eternally grateful to Spanner for teaching me a valuable lesson in life – that gambling is a mug's game unless you are a real expert. I am not and never will be.

This is what happened to teach me my lesson.

I was on my first or second detachment to El Adem in Libya, well-documented elsewhere. Aircraft servicing work can involve long periods of boredom. You were always waiting for something: planes to land, planes to get ready, planes to take off/park/service. Away from the airfield, you were waiting for other necessities: meals, beverages, food, pay. You got used to waiting but games like cards helped pass the time. So, as we set out for El Adem, I found myself in an apparently innocent card school of four, with Spanner and two others, both married blokes, one with a couple of kids. They were good lads, a bit older than myself but all three of us were way out of our depths when playing cards with Spanner. Seamlessly he organized that we should keep our four together in the same card school over the two weeks we were away. We needn't use actual money, he told us, just a points system of plus and minus after each hand. We could then settle up at the end of the detachment – all ok lads? We all agreed and he set the rules, which seemed more than fair.

It all appeared above any suspicion but there was just one drawback – we were playing the deadly game of *three-card brag*. If you've ever played it you will know that unless you get everything agreed and understood right from the start, things can go wrong and trouble comes. In our case, Spanner smoothly introduced the bidding levels, which all seemed very acceptable, no wild bets, maximum fifty pence, I think, from memory. After a day or so, with one or two minor wins by each of the three of us, we all seemed to be slightly down with only Spanner up, and this became the pattern over the next few days.

It took about four days for it to dawn on me that Spanner's system of playing three-card brag was different to ours. When we looked at our hands, if we had a good one we went on, a bad one was thrown and an average one was sweated out to 'brag' about, eventually either winning or losing. But Spanner played all his hands 'blind', whereas we all looked at ours. That meant we were putting twice as much as he was (blind hands pay half as much into the kitty as seen hands). By the time he had worn us down to only one opponent against him, the others having 'folded', he had studied us and could read our faces and the clues and measure our anxiety as to whether we really did have a good hand or not. Eventually, when he picked up and looked at his hand, he could then make a measured decision as to whether to prolong our agony with another bid or fold to allow us to win. But his stake was lower than ours had been all through, thus his losses were less than ours. By the time I realised what was happening we were all in debt to Spanner. I was in the middle of the other two but it was a fair amount to lose in those days, about £25 I think.

It took a lot of courage for me to switch my system to his and a lot more of a learning curve to play it, but gradually the tide turned and I began to pull back. The other two continued to play the same way, occasionally winning, sometimes a good one, but still steadily losing overall. By the end of the two-week detachment, when settle-up time came, I owed Spanner £9, a considerable reduction from £25, but the other two were in dire straits. The one with the kids owed him £73 and the other £115, the latter being forced to give Spanner an IOU and pay him back, unbeknown to his wife, over a matter of weeks at £20 per week until the debt was cleared.

To say I learnt a valuable lesson on that detachment is a massive understatement. I was badly out of my depth but fortunately realised that I was and always would be cannon-fodder for people like Spanner, who knew exactly what they were doing whereas I didn't.

If his card-playing was excellent, his absolute forte was darts. He fascinated me playing darts, not just because he was good but in the way he finished games. Hitting doubles was a particular skill but his party piece was when his score reached 32. Invariably his first dart went just inside the double, leaving him 16, same performance again leaving him with 8. When he shaped up to double four, you got used to what was coming. He would just miss double four, scoring a single four to leave four. As the dart hit that single number he would swing round to anyone who was watching, or just his opponent and say, 'Double two – I never miss double two' and would immediately plant it smack in the middle of double two. I never recall seeing him miss it over many games; he could do it sober, half-cut or blind drunk, it made no difference. I've never seen anyone else do that.

As he had a reputation for never chasing women, unlike the rest of us, he cheerfully bore the brunt of our sarcasm on the subject. Spanner was in his mid-twenties and it was alleged he had never even been near a woman, which he neither confirmed nor denied, always laughing it off with a self-deprecating joke. So imagine our surprise at events one weekend when we all trooped off to the Isle of Wight to celebrate our mate Tom's twenty-first birthday, one of our number who was actually from that island.

At this point I must mention 'Bagman' syndrome. A Bagman was the derogatory nickname given to those who, at every opportunity, went home or wherever for the weekend, clutching their weekend bag. Quite why they joined up in the first place was a mystery. Like homing pigeons they were dots in the distance minutes after finishing work on Fridays, only to re-appear on Mondays or late Sunday evenings. We had a number of bagmen from the Isle of Wight, although Tom wasn't one. I went once or twice to the island, but never discovered the attraction of the place.

At the party that weekend on the island there were only a few spare women – nurses, I think – invited to even up the numbers, but they were heavily outnumbered. You had to be quick that night and I hadn't had enough to drink, so I dipped out. But Spanner, of all people, didn't. Well, I mean – Spanner! His belle was a big, fat woman who looked like she was auditioning for a part in *Hiawatha, the movie* – by that I mean she was dressed from head to toe in a huge multi-coloured tent-like garment, I think they called it a kaftan; she reminded me a poor man's Mama Cass.

Adorning a well-lived-in brown face, she had lank brown hair down over her shoulders – and she smoked a pipe! We were all amazed as she and Spanner seemed strangely but quickly drawn to each other, getting closer and closer, even swapping pipe and fags temporarily in an apparently peace-love trance they shared together. Move over John and Yoko. Before the end of the evening, they had both disappeared, to where we didn't know, but the next morning, just before we were due to leave to return to camp via the ferry and train, Spanner suddenly re-appeared.

I say Spanner, but in actual fact, this was a new version of the old one. There was a certain cool, contented air about him, his eyes shone as though he had seen the promised land – apparently he had! He told us, very sincerely, that he had just had the best night of his life. In his own words, she had 'sucked him in and blown him out in bubbles'. We were all stunned, to put it mildly. When we pushed him to find out the gory details of exactly what she had done, all he would say was 'everything!' – with a glazed look on his face – but he would not elaborate.

It really confirmed to us that this had been the first time for Spanner. He was quiet and even vaguely conscientious at work for weeks, acting with a certain calm and smugness, but gradually he returned to his old, idle self. He made it perfectly clear that he considered the night had been a 'one-off' and added that Hiawatha had apparently said so too. Consequently, Spanner never showed any more inclination in her direction, despite our exhortations to get off his arse and seek her out for another mind-blower – or whatever blower she had used. It seemed as if he had climbed Everest once – as in 'been there, done that' – and there was no need to repeat the feat, which puzzled us somewhat, although, of course, he was always completely indolent. To find her again would have required some effort on his part, so no chance there, and that's the way it stayed.

I often wonder what became of him. In a normal civvy job he was virtually unemployable but I quite liked Spanner. He was not stupid, he could be even be quite witty on occasions, and he had a dry sense of humour I liked.

When I left the RAF in 1972, Spanner was exactly as I had met him about four years previously – lazy, smoking for Britain, drinking, half-living in pubs and tight-fisted as ever.

Where are you now, Spanner?

Not with Hiawatha, surely?

21. Lawbreakin'

'So...' the smartass RAF Police corporal sniggered. 'What law are you breaking, then? My first thought was amazement. How did he know? Had someone ratted on me? Who knew all the facts? Now I was really in it, at least with the RAF Police and possibly and more importantly, the *real* Police.

I had been stopped at the barrier coming into our camp – the infamous 'Deeps Guard' as it was known. 'Deeps' referred to the treacherous, creeky, smelly waters around the island that served as our home, the RAF station where I lived and worked. Sometimes, depending on the time of the day/night/week/month the barrier was up and sometimes it was down, but this time it was down and I had been stopped coming back onto the island.

I was having substantial car trouble and after having my Triumph Herald welded up at the garage in the local village was returning to camp, when I was stopped by this jobsworth Snowdrop. It should be added that, with one or two notable exceptions, we hated the RAF Police. By *we* I mean just about everyone in the RAF. For their part they hated us all in return, but the Plods particularly disliked the 'wild bunch' of us who worked on the aircraft, who they regarded as scruffy and undisciplined (about right) and always ripe for settling old scores.

He sauntered round my car, casually kicking the tyres. (I was once told that this is how to tell a person who knows nothing about cars, when buying one. Clueless as to what to look for, he kicks the tyres, as if knowledgeable). Well – I had no insurance or MOT but the tax disc was in its last month of duty, so... what was the answer to his question? What law was I breaking?

The truth was that I'd had an accident a few weeks earlier in which the large bonnet of the Herald sustained damage that required some welding. If you don't know, the bonnet and front wings of a Herald were all one complete unit, they hinged on the end of two big wrought iron arms that came forward from the metal chassis of the car. So a collision anywhere in the front area of the Herald was not good due to the spin-off to other normally separate parts. I had hit the front hard on one side and bent the front of the bonnet near one wing. Having got that welded up, I was returning to the camp to make further repairs myself before attempting another well-overdue MOT. Smartass repeated the question, this time more emphatically and sarcastically, but generously gave me a clue.

'What is supposed to be on the front and back of all cars to identify them? What have you got on the back but not on the front?' I suddenly remembered forgetting to screw the front number plate back on for my short journey to the garage in the village and back. I explained my actions to the fairly disinterested Snowdrop, omitting the illegal aspects. He must have been in a good mood that day as he gave me a half-hearted wigging and promised to do me 'next time' if he caught me without number plates again. With all the deference and thanks I could muster, I returned to the block to relate the story humorously to the lads.

Now that the car looked ok (well it would with the number plate on) I had another problem in that the newly-welded complete bonnet would not sit right down and could not be secured by the clips low down on either wing. This was because one of the heavy metal forks holding the pivot for the complete bonnet unit took the impact of the collision, and was now pushed back and up several inches out of line. How would I get it back in place?

There was a block of pre-cast concrete garages near the accommodation we lived in. They were supposed to be for rent, but hardly anyone bothered, even though the charges were ridiculously low, about £1.50 a month I think. But lately a few cheekier ones of us – was I the ringleader? Yes, I possibly was – had commandeered the lockable garages, keeping our cars in them as if we rented them.

One hot Sunday afternoon, after a few lunchtime pints, a couple of mates and I set to work to straighten out my bent fork. We removed the bonnet and positioned the Herald in the garage I was using, with the fork directly under the front top concrete span of the garage door. From somewhere we obtained a metal girder about four feet long, placed it vertically over the end of the fork, running up to the roof of the garage at the front and, with the aid of bricks and an expanding bottle-jack, began to exert downward pressure on the fork, which required pushing back down about three to four inches.

First of all the tyres started to go slowly down with the pressure. We stopped this with bricks, but then, to my horror, the front concrete spar across the top of the garage began to lift. The garages were built in a block of pre-cast concrete, all bolted together, and the increasing pressure we exerted was taking up the slack of all the bolts. Our plan wasn't working and bit by bit the garages on either side were beginning to creak and groan under the strain.

One of my good mates, Tom, who was helping me, was a right head-banger. On a nutcase scale where 1 is normal and sensible, and 10 is certifiable and should be locked up, in those days I would modestly describe myself as 5, after drinking 6 or even 7 but Tom was 7 – 8 normally, bordering on 9 when he had been drinking. He had that afternoon and he had control of the bottle-jack. On he went, click, click, click went the ratchet and, from a safe distance, I could see several other garages on either side beginning to creak as well as those immediately next to mine. I suddenly had visions of the whole lot coming down, with precious cars inside being irreparably damaged, and the financial consequences began to dawn on me.

I told Tom to stop but he took no notice, going for a 10 rating that afternoon. Click, click, click, he went on, insisting that it was working. I wasn't convinced but as he went on I could see the fork was, at last, beginning to move down. I thought he would never stop – click, click, click – I couldn't look but at last he announced the fork was now in line with its partner and we gratefully dismantled everything. I could almost hear the grateful sighing of the garages as they returned to normal. We put the bonnet back on and it fitted properly again. Phew!

Several weeks later, I had been on the early shift at work, a five am start, and was returning after breakfast about ten o'clock when I was told to get down to the dreaded Station Head Quarters (SHQ) asap. There had been a phone call ordering my urgent presence and I was to report to the Provost Officer, he in charge of all things administrative. I was told my mate Steve had already been similarly summoned and was on his way. As SHQ was the shiniest place on camp, and we came from the scruffiest part, SHQ invited much danger if we dared to visit there. There was much nudging and amusement in my direction as I vainly sought the reason for my summons. No wiser, I headed towards SHQ via the block where I lived, in an urgent attempt to smarten myself up.

I arrived at the Provost's office in time to see Steve being marched out. He winked broadly at me, which re-assured me somewhat, but I still had no idea why I was there. I was marched in by the same eagle-eyed RAF Snowdrop who had spotted my absent numberplate. He looked euphoric. The Provost Officer, Hambleton (nicknamed Humblebum due to his Uriah Heep demeanour) was a complete prat of the first order, well known for his bumbling, inefficient manner over the most straightforward of tasks. He began by asking me if I knew why I was there. When I replied negatively he explained that a snap inspection of the garages had revealed a number of cars illegally parked inside them. Was this my car, registration number, etc? When I confirmed that it was, he demanded to know why it was illegally parked there.

'Well sir,' I began, making it up as I went along. 'My car is off the road at the moment, needing some work doing for the MOT, and as parts have been removed I put them and the car into the garage earlier this week as I didn't want the parts pilfered. I can see I should have asked permission sir, and I apologise, but it was for security purposes'. I tried to make the last bit sound as if I was helping the Police to maintain law and order. In truth, the car had been there months, perhaps even over a year.

'It's off the road, now is it?' asked Humblebum. 'You havn't been driving it at all?' I had to be careful now, as Smartarse Eagle-Eyes had seen me driving it at the barrier.

'Well, sir,' I said earnestly. 'The only time I drove it was recently, when I took it off camp for a visit to a garage workshop to get some welding done before the MOT.' I was marched out while they checked whether this was ok, at which point the Snowdrop hissed in my ear that he knew I had been driving it round camp illegally for months (he was right). I was marched back in.

'All right, McGregor,' announced Humblebum officiously. 'I have checked with the civil authorities and they agree with your version.

However, your admission that you used the garage without permission is just not acceptable and I am going to show you that you cannot do things like that without permission. With immediate effect you will take over the rental of the garage and as a punishment, I am fining you four weeks back rent.'

It was hard not to burst out laughing, it was so ridiculous! I felt like posing an effeminate stance and saying, Kenneth Williams-like, 'Oh, no, please sir – not *that* punishment. I can't take it!'

I was marched out by the Snowdrop, muttering under his breath that he estimated I had been using the garage for at least three months (it was more than that really) and that he had also seen me driving my car round the camp. He had, of course, but he couldn't prove it, so all-in-all the whole thing was a scream – you couldn't make it up.

Four more of us in our close circle were similarly *done* by the snap garage inspection and that evening we all had a great laugh about it over a few beers: we had a 'gay' competition over who could do the best Humblebum impersonation.

I finally got the Herald legally back on the road several weeks later and had a few more months of successfully driving it before I crashed it again, this time irredeemably. It was a good car but too fast for me. Although I was learning the art of driving a speedy car safely, I still had a long way to go!

22. The Twins

I wish I had learned to sail. It was just that at that period of my life, 1967 to 1972, there were so many other distractions, especially at the Sailing Club on the island where our RAF home was situated. Discos playing our type of music, in places like the Sailing Club, were just coming in and with a DJ who could put it over well – and we had one or two in our number – we had a rich source of entertainment. Now all we needed was young women – lots of them.

It was a great spot, the Sailing Club, with a long bar and plate glass windows that looked out over the harbour, where small boats came and went all the time – very picturesque. The trouble was that the Club was not easily accessible to the general public, so the required young women had to be brought in, in ones, twos or any number really. This story is about two *big* distractions...

It was on a hot Saturday lunchtime in July 1970, with the club half-full of mainly lusty young airmen, that *the twins* wandered in on their own. Nobody seemed to know exactly where they had come from or how they had got there, but their entrance, well, 'WOW!' was the effect. They were quite stunning. Aged about nineteen, five feet two-ish, they had short blonde hair bobbed a la Lulu in her 'Shout' era. These two were bright, pretty, blue-eyed, vivacious, open-faced, mischievous, smiley and – *very* sexy.

I'm sure you get the picture!

With their tight white summer tops stretched over generous fulsome bra-less boobs and pink hot pants, revealing acres of milky white fleshy thighs and lovely slender legs leading down to the high heels they tottered in on – can you imagine the effect? Do I need to explain what hot pants are? A sort of cross between tight-fitting legless shorts and a pair of M&S stretchy knickers is about the best description I can muster. They were worn, well, tight and stretchy, revealing exciting female curves, guaranteed to put any hearty young man's blood pressure up a bit, especially inflaming a certain part of his body.

Bearing in mind that there is a popular, albeit hugely unlikely, male fantasy of doing exciting things with a pair of female twins, the effect of this dynamic, absolutely identical twosome's show-stopping entrance into our testosterone-charged world was devastating. Within seconds they were surrounded, drinks bought, chairs and knees generously provided, stubbly male chins scraped from the ground to whence they had dropped. The atmosphere in the club had been considerably brightened.

For the next few weeks they seemed to appear at every social occasion, never appearing to go out with any one – or two – young airmen separately or 'normally' that I heard of. They chose a different lucky one each time on an ad-hoc, short-term, whoever-they-fancied-at-the-time basis. The stories circulated quickly that if the mood took them, then brief, exciting, all-your-birthdays-coming-at-once action often took place in the car park, along the shore, behind the club, even in the gents, it was reported. In public they loved dancing and were very good at it, in a hugely sexually erotic come-and-get-it way, just to sit and watch the two together in perfect time with each other was a welcome diversion during a torridly hot summer.

Me? Alas no, I never seemed to be able to move quickly enough when they suddenly appeared, usually as if from nowhere. There were plenty of elbows in your ribs when they were around and in any case I seem to remember being otherwise engaged (lustily, I mean, certainly not betrothally-promised) at the time, but a couple of my close mates did briefly sample what was on offer.

Geordie was a good-looking, pencil-slim paramedic, who didn't work with us on the aircraft but we played football, drank and socialised together. He was a good mate. He had jet black floppy hair, always down over his eyes, which seemed to appeal to women, a bit Bryan Ferry-ish, and I suppose the fact that one night he was in uniform on duty worked perfectly in his favour. This particular night, when the twins had just arrived, he had picked up some chips (wrapped) and wanted a pint to wash them down on his evening supper break.

I cannot remember the twins' names, we just called them *the twins* and this particular occasion one of them took a shine to lucky old Geordie. She had her arm round his waist in no time, admiring his uniform, straightening his tie and stroking his hair, so it was no surprise when he came over and whispered to me, 'Mac, I'm just slipping off back to the block, cover for me if the Sarge comes looking for me,' and the two of them abruptly disappeared. Her twin appeared totally unconcerned; she was currently involved in a two-way groping situation in a far-off dark corner of the bar with a huge gorilla-like airman who was earnestly making the most of his chance – as you would.

Twenty minutes later, Geordie's presence was sought by his sergeant, who came looking for him. Being one of his mates, I offered, honestly as it happened, the news that he *had* been there and that perhaps he had gone 'off camp' for his supper? Chips maybe?

'Tell him to get back soon if you see him,' was the curt reply. As soon as the coast was clear, I jumped into my car and sped back to the block, five minutes away. Geordie lived in a different room to ours, much smaller and in this case, dark and fairly private. His room was upstairs, first bed on the left, surrounded for privacy by 6ft high lockers.

I quietly opened the door. Inside the room it was semi-darkness. At first I thought no-one was there but then I heard a slight grunting and rustling. Feeling like a perverted peeping Tom, I crept around to the entrance and from the end of the bed I observed two naked figures on the bed, one on top of the other. Geordie's skinny, bare white bum was enthusiastically pumping up and down, with the twin's legs emerging either side, wrapped round his own. What ruined this tender love scene, however, was the fact that she was eating his chips over his shoulder about as enthusiastically as he was pumping himself into her. Neither seemed to notice me and for a moment I considered leaving them to their sexual and gastric pleasures, but I was a loyal servant of the Queen and, well, duty and friendship called. Tiptoeing up to the side of the bed, feeling like some sort of voyeur, I tapped my mate's arm.

'Geordie, your Sarge is looking for you.'

'Is he? What did you tell him?' asked Casanova over his shoulder, pausing briefly, with his beau totally ignoring me and continuing to dine.

'I said you might have gone off camp. That was only ten minutes ago. He didn't seem too bothered, just to tell you to get back if I saw you.' He seemed vaguely relieved

'Thanks, Mac, you're a pal' he acknowledged, then continued his passionate thrustings, nodding dismissively over his shoulder.

I can take a hint and duly departed, shaking my head in disbelief at what I had just witnessed – the path of true lust.

The other story involving the twins occurred at a section 'do' – a social evening with drink, food and entertainment, again in the Sailing Club. All members of our squadron were invited with their wives or girlfriends, such events usually happened once or twice a year. Our Commanding Officer and his wife were invited as guests of honour and normally it was a good social occasion with copious amounts of free food and booze, an opportunity for a knees-up with one of our resident DJs playing our sort of music.

However, on this occasion the twins were in town, well-oiled and mischievous. RAF officers are, to a man, a breed apart. They have a certain bearing that marks them out as leaders. Our own CO was a pleasant, popular youngish officer in his early 30s and his lovely young wife was a few months pregnant and just beginning to show it. They arrived late and an alcohol-encouraged cheer went up as they entered the large bar of the Club. They stood, smiling shyly together, acknowledging their warm welcome, when one of the twins suddenly appeared at the officer's elbow. She turned sideways towards him and buried her head in his neck, but it was her hand that we all saw as she gripped his crutch firmly, rubbing it as she did so.

With true heroic presence of mind that such men would always show in such an emergency, he took her wrist and offered it gallantly to the nearest airman, who gratefully grabbed it. Twisting away from the playful twin, he led his wife over to some senior figures and their wives as if nothing had happened, almost demonstrating that he was used to such minor occurrences. His wife appeared a little startled, as though someone had let off an unexpected firework, but she recovered and also seemed to take it all in her stride, as though that sort of thing was to be expected from the ranks. Despite the drink, we were all shocked. No-one would have dared to set up such an incident, that sort of disrespect would not have entered our minds. We were all certain it was a typical spur-of-the-moment fun thing, the type of lively devilment the twins seemed to delight in if the mood took them.

They were only around for a few weeks that summer but they certainly livened up the place. The twins disappeared as quickly as they had come and no-one knew where to. Rumours circulated that they had moved on and were now entertaining the Navy. Stationed near Portsmouth, as we were, there would be plenty of work for them to do there.

If entertaining the troops was their mission, that summer they certainly entertained us!

23. The Bermuda Triangle

'Mac, it's fookin' Christmas! I've put yours and my names down on the list together, we're third to go. Bermuda, here we come – it'll be fookin' great Mac, you'll see. Mike 'n' Kathy are magic!'

Dave was a short-arse, short-haired, blunt-speaking Mancunian mate of mine, a relatively normal human being until he neared a football ground where Manchester United were playing. Then, in a dramatic Jekyll-and-Hyde transformation, he became a real football hooligan, a yob, a madman, almost ready to kill for the cause in the name of the Stretford End. On this occasion, however, he was full of ale and blunt northern rhetoric.

The sensational news had just broken was that the 'Navex', or Navigational Exercise to give it its proper name, was changing from Singapore to Bermuda. The training crews on our station had to complete a long haul exercise over oceans to different parts of the world, and back and we ground crew were allowed on such trips as 'jollies' to help out where needed, usually just two of us per trip. The Bermuda run was a direct flight out there, incorporating an uncomfortable fourteen-odd hour trip across the Atlantic, staying the night in Bermuda in a fabulous hotel called *The Castle Harbour*, which overlooked the glorious bay.

The next day the Navex flew on to Larges, an American Air Force base in the Azores islands in Mid Atlantic. There we could enjoy our Yank friends' superb hospitality for a second night – they really know how to treat their servicemen – before finally flying back to complete a wonderful triangular Navex; *The Bermuda Triangle*, as it became affectionately known.

Dave had a particular vested interest in this trip when it was announced, as his aunt and uncle actually lived in Bermuda and he had never been to see them. The story went that they were a homely couple from Lancashire who both worked at a swanky hotel in the centre of Manchester. Every year a wealthy American doctor from New York used to visit the hotel and steadily, over a period of some years, took a shine to Mike, eventually asking if he and Kathy would like to come and work for him in Bermuda. On this idyllic island was the American's holiday residence, a mansion where he lived for about twelve weeks a year. A lovely bungalow went with the job, in the grounds of the huge sprawling estate at one end of the main island of Bermuda. Mike and Kathy had been there for several years and were very happy – and Dave was itching to get out there to see for himself how the other half live. Now was his chance, courtesy of Her Majesty, with me in tow.

There was another, slightly devious, chancy element to the trip. Hercules aircraft were very airworthy – good, safe aircraft that are still flying today. But there was always a chance, albeit slim, that somewhere abroad – somewhere exotic, perhaps? – they might just develop a fault that would take some time to repair. Perhaps somewhere there were no spares and parts would have to be flown in specially? Where a few days in a paradise like Bermuda could be enjoyed while you waited for help to arrive – a bit fanciful, eh? But you can dream, can't you?

Dave was an airframes mechanic, the worst of all aircraft trades in my book. There were six aircraft trades, airframes and engines, known colloquially as 'heavies', the other four being electrics, radio, radar and navigation instruments, these last four referred to scathingly as 'fairies' by the heavy mob. I was a 'fairy', as I was a radio mechanic. There was always good-natured rivalry and ribaldry between heavies and fairies. The former would come into the crew room having been working outside in all weathers, swearing and cursing, only to see us fairies sitting round in comfort, drinking coffee and playing cards.

We endured taunts like, 'The next day you fuggin' lot work'll be the first for years', to which such unabashed wit we would inevitably retort airily, 'We get paid for what we know, not for what we do.'

That usually had the desired effect and was a cue for more appalling language. But in truth airframes was an awful job. Piles (haemorrhoids, I mean!) were an occupational hazard because the job often entailed lying upside down on cold concrete 'pans' under aircraft in order to work on them. Mancunian Dave bore his workload with a certain northern grit but our heavy/fairy relationship was good to take as balanced servicing crew on such flights.

Our turn on the Bermuda run took some time to happen, being postponed for a couple of months and Dave's 'fookin' Christmas' prediction was almost true. We took off on 9th December 1970 for our marathon trip across the Atlantic. Hercules flights are noisy, boring and comfortless. They are, after all, basic transport aircraft built to carry heavy goods or paratroopers but not *real* passengers. Seating was on nylon webbing strung between tubular steel rods, bloody uncomfortable after a while. After fourteen hours in a Herc you knew all about it. It took hours for the vibration and noise to leave your body, but this day we arrived safely in Bermuda in mid-afternoon.

When we landed Dave did his after-flight checks. These usually took about half an hour but he found me after ten minutes, buzzing with excitement. 'We're U/S!' he announced with heavy satisfaction. U/S was aircraft-speak for unserviceable, meaning a fault that had to be rectified before the plane could take off again. He led me proudly down to the huge main wheels of the Hercules, where a small leak of hydraulic oil could be seen running from a seal down the side of the brake unit onto the pan. The news spread round the aircrew like wildfire and they were as excited as we were, all well aware of the repercussions. Well, *nearly* all of them were excited. The captain and senior figure on our trip was Squadron Leader Hayes, nicknamed 'Granny' Hayes for his old-woman attitude to service matters. In this case, he curtly dismissed Dave's U/S claim.

'That's nothing to worry about; we'll take that in the morning'.

My Lancastrian friend pointed out, rather bluntly, I thought, that there was no such thing as a leak 'within limits'.

'A leak is a *leak* ... sir.' Dave pronounced it emphatically, as though delivering sentence, adding the 'sir' grudgingly, but Hayes would have none of it.

'No, we'll take that tomorrow.' Shaking his head, he strode firmly away, his disconsolate crew in tow. Crestfallen at this heaven-sent gift being so casually dismissed, we were somewhat mollified to be taken to our lovely hotel, although we had no time to enjoy it. Dave immediately rang Mike and Kathy who exhorted us to get to them by taxi as soon as possible. As we only had one night in Bermuda, they wanted to take us out and show us around. I whipped off my sweaty, sticky uniform and jumped in the shower, which was over the bath behind a curtain. At that point, an unforgivable thing happened, one which for some awful reason, is still etched in my memory. I was showering and shampooing when a disgusting smell reached me. I jerked back the curtain to find Dave sitting on the loo, inches away, grinning up at me.

'Snap this off for me, Mac!' he grinned.

'You filthy pig! Couldn't you have waited!'

I should have known. Although a good mate, Dave could be very *earthy* at times, to put it politely.

The story improves now, you'll be pleased to know.

Suitably abluted and cleanly dressed, we jumped into a taxi and drove through the beautiful, green, leafy countryside of the main island. In case you don't know, Bermuda is made up of several long, narrow islands that run east/west with lovely pink coral beaches on the north side and rocky mini-inlets along the south side. As we're in the mood for travel information, Bermuda is not in the Caribbean, as most people imagine, it is way out into the Atlantic, 500 miles due south of New York, and it is a British island, with British policemen (in Bermuda shorts).

We arrived at Mike and Kathy's beautiful bungalow and they told the taxi driver to wait while we all enjoyed a long, cooling drink, chatting nineteen to the dozen. I felt as though I had known them all my life. Then this very entertaining older couple took us out to the main town of Hamilton on a sort of upmarket pub crawl round lovely bars, clubs and a restaurant where we ate. They told us how they came to be living on this beautiful island, the story being a wonderful combination of hard work and good luck.

Their boss and landlord was reputedly one of the richest men in the USA, a doctor of some description, I seem to remember, but he travelled extensively and gave lectures around the world. His 'hobby', if you can call it that, was the study of water-based creatures, he was 'big' in the New York aquarium.

At regular intervals throughout the evening and night, either Mike or Kathy would pose the statement, 'it's a shame you're not here for longer, there's so much to do and see here'. That may not be verbatim but it was the gist of it. Dave's face was a study as the evening wore on. Admittedly, a lot of drink was consumed but a sort of gritty irritation (determination?) took over his normally expressionless features.

Eventually we ended up back at the bungalow, where after a few more drinks we had to say our goodbyes and reluctantly take our leave, with promises to return soon. After what seemed no time at all, back at the hotel an alarm clock went off in our hotel room. Then the telephone rang, to remind us of our duties, calling us to serve Her Majesty. Our heads ached and we were very short of sleep but we were well used to such minor inconveniences. Swearing and coffee helped enormously in such situations.

We were taken out to our aircraft to prepare it for the flight. My checks took about ten minutes, if I did them slowly, whereas Dave's took at least an hour. After doing mine, Dave asked me to give him a hand by going up onto the flight deck and pumping the brakes; fairly routine stuff. Up on the flight deck, sitting in his seat and pretending to be the captain, I pumped the brakes as requested. Did I hear a muffled shout from somewhere deep down below? Descending the steps from the aircraft, I could see Dave's feet sticking out from underneath the wheel well. Also near him was a large, rapidly spreading pool of hydraulic oil. He scrambled out breathlessly, his normally dead-pan features radiant.

'What happened?' I asked.

Dave shrugged casually but not concealing his excitement.

'Seal must have given way under normal brake pressure,' was his grave summary. Five minutes later, our engineer arrived to do his pre-flight checks. He was barely able to conceal his delight on discovering the news. The rest of the crew arrived and were in turn pleasantly surprised and not displeased. But of course, there is always one, and this one was *not* best pleased. Hayes interrogated Dave carefully, until he was sure of his facts.

'So you carried out your normal brake safety checks?' *Pause, stare.* 'And you believe the seal gave way under pressure?' *Further grave pause, narrowed eyes.* 'Causing an excessive leak?'

Hayes sounded like he was at the Old Bailey.

'Yes sir,' agreed Dave, solemnly nodding.

There was silence; we all held our breath.

'Right!' announced the suddenly decisive captain, swinging into action as if in the trenches. He barked orders out to all around about sending emergency signals to the UK, requesting permission to do this and that and telling the co-pilot to re-book the hotel rooms until further notice. All that was needed for our part was a new brake unit to be ordered, which Dave could fit with my help. The only problem was where would a new unit come from? If from the UK, as was likely, it would take two or three days to arrive – how sad!

Bingo! Three bells appeared in a line on our fruit machine of life, as back we went to the fantastic Castle Harbour Hotel, where large-girthed Americans waddled around with huge cigars talking golf, with their lined-but-tanned wives discussing clothes, hair and jewellery and criticising each other and their husbands loudly.

Dave and I paid a very profitable visit to the co-pilot's bedroom, where we were issued with 108 US dollars, the currency of Bermuda, which represented four days 'LOA' or Local Overseas Allowance at twenty-seven dollars per day. This LOA ostensibly enabled one to exist materially in whatever local conditions one found oneself, the amount being laid down in Queen's Regulations somewhere. Our co-pilot knew where – and played his part to perfection.

Guess where we headed? Not the nearest bar, as was our wont usually but straight to Mike and Kathy, who couldn't believe our news. They were as good as their word and gave us a wonderful time. Their hospitality knew no bounds. As eating out in Bermuda was expensive (hence the twenty-seven dollars per day) these two lovely people showed us generous Northern hospitality, insisting we ate all our meals with them all the time.

Only taxis and buses were allowed on Bermuda in those days as transport, no private cars, but everyone aged twelve and over rode little automatic mopeds. We immediately hired two and off we went. We played golf, badly, on fantastic courses, swam in fabulous warm seas, toured the sun-soaked islands from one end to the other on our little two-wheelers and generally had a ball. Our overall host from over the pond we never met, but our American doctor friend had sealed off some of his little inlets from the sea on the rocky south side of his land, to provide breeding grounds for various forms of sea-life. It was absolutely delightful to move along them seeing one-year-old terrapins in one, two-year-olds in the next, etc, along with grouper fish, angel fish, baby octopus, etc. The list was endless. It was fascinating just to watch Mike and Kathy feeding them all. It was, quite simply, a holiday never to forget. Oh, sorry, I don't mean holiday – I meant a working vacation!

A few more minor details – sadly, the aircraft bringing out our spare brake unit went U/S in flight itself with engine trouble and had to stop off in The Azores for repair. We finally made it back to the UK on 20th December, arriving in light snow, having enjoyed twelve wonderful days in the sunshine in Bermuda, with tans to match. That went down well with the rest of lads! The icy cold, curious, envious faces of our ground crew mates as we disembarked from our trip to paradise told us we had many questions to answer and, over numerous pints, we did our best.

As it was Christmas we had bought our loved ones presents with a 'Bermuda' flavour wherever possible. Several trips to the co-pilot's room ensured we had plenty of money to spend on such gifts and souvenirs. Mike and Kathy would take nothing from us, they said they had Utopia themselves already and told us they were just grateful to have some UK visitors. It was expensive to get to Bermuda in those days.

Anything else you want to know? Well, I only know the same as Granny Hayes – the seal gave way under pressure – and despite how many pints the little Mancunian sod drank, that remained his story. He stuck to it, so it must be true. Don't you agree?

24. Shiny Stories – AOCs

You remember the bit about the 'real' Air Force, the one where they paint the grass green and coal black – ever heard the expression 'bullshit baffles brains'? Well, the time that affected most airmen like that was the dreaded 'AOCs', which stood for 'Air Officer Commanding's Inspection', usually carried out annually. In our case, it was always in May, when our station was as pretty as a picture, being full of pink and white almond blossom from the hundreds of trees lining the roads around the camp. At our scruffy end of the camp, where we got on with the real work an Air Force is meant for, the big man did not visit, fortunately. We made a token effort to keep those who were in charge of our outfit happy but we all dreaded being caught for the AOC's parade.

This involved being drilled for a few weeks prior to the visit by the most feared person in any airman's life, the SWO (pronounced as in *swoe*) which stood for the Station Warrant Officer, his equivalent rank in the army being the Regimental Sergeant Major. I haven't got a clue about the Navy – why would I? Twice I got 'caught' for AOC's – more of that later – and had to endure a couple of hours practising marching and even worse as far as we were concerned, presentation of arms training. I know that as an active serviceman I should be acquainted with arms, etc, but I was employed for 'black box changing', not farting about with rifles – and these buggers had bayonets on, very sharp ones too ("they don't like it up 'em," do they Corporal Jones?)

So we all put our Best Blues on, our number one uniform or 'number ones' – softer material, longer jacket with pockets, belt, peaked twat-hat, etc – and toddled along to risk the wrath of the SWO, especially if your hair was longer than you could get away with. The SWO's priority was to knock sixty of us into a smart little unit of three spaced out lines, twenty in each one, standing side by side, all looking to the front. The AOC's small plane would taxi in to the visiting 'pan', where we were all lined up to meet him. The aircraft stopped in front of us, cut its engines, the door opened and 'He' came down the steps. As he did so, the SWO thundered,

'Royal Air Force Thorney Island Guard of Honour... Pre... sent *Arms!*'

It wasn't that hard really, if you had been through basic training, when we had done this presenting arms with heavy .303 rifles, but by now standard issue was the much lighter SLR's; although the bayonets were sharper. Standing to attention holding the neck of the rifle (reading this back I almost sound as though I know what I'm talking about!) you sort of flick it upwards and catch the edge of the butt in your right hand, bringing the left over to steady the vicious end. Then, gripping the rifle firmly in the right, you transfer the whole thing across in front of you, bayonet dangerously around head height as you steady the whole thing with your left hand, which is extended, pointing upwards. The right foot comes back and at right angles close to the left and you are 'presenting arms'. Just what the fug it's all for I have no idea but that's the drill we all practised for a few weeks before 'God' came. Then he went off for his short tour round the brilliantly shining camp – well, most of it – before going into the officers' mess for a few drinkypoos and then buggering off back from whence he came. What a farce! *The Annual Rain Dance* some called it.

But this one particular year, 1970 I think, was spectacular. As the saying goes, there's always one, and this year we had a pearler in our midst – Jenkins, from South Wales. Jenkins was firmly the lowest of the low in the RAF – a TAG, which stood for Trade Assistant General. That meant you had no trade at all, you were waiting for a course to come up because you had either been thrown off or failed a previous one. In effect, you were a dogsbody, fair game for anything menial or demeaning, like washing aircraft, sweeping and cleaning along with anyone who happened to be in the guardhouse.

As Jenkins was quite fit and had apparently at one time boxed for the RAF, they put him in the gym to do stuff nobody else would do. There he was the butt of various RAF comedians who took delight in winding him up, often phoning him up using stupid voices. This internal phone misuse was a common RAF game, utilised when boredom set in. One morning, after he had been exasperated by several such calls, the phone rang and a well-spoken voice said,

'Is that the gym? Ah, good morning, Squadron Leader Hastings-Scott here. I'd like to complain about the state of the Officers' mess tennis courts...'

'Piss off, Robbie,' Jenkins abruptly replied. 'I've got work to do, even if you haven't,' before slamming the phone down.

Then an awful thought hit him, and he grabbed the internal phone book. There, under 'H', he saw 'Hastings-Scott, officer i/c Control Tower'. Hands shaking, he dialled the number and mumbled his deep apologies to the shocked Hastings-Scott, who was about to phone the guardroom alleging insubordination in the ranks, but fortunately let it go. But that was Jenkins ... and to our surprise he was picked for AOCs.

He really shouldn't have been picked, as he was clumsy and made elementary mistakes during marching practice. But we all chivvied him along and although the SWO swore at him a few times, he kept Jenkins in our unit. However, after one practice session the Welsh flanker pulled his bayonet off the top of the rifle (a fairly routine twist and pull operation) and in doing so managed to stab himself in the cheek. Result? Blood everywhere. It really did serve as a warning but despite this he was there on the big day. I'm not sure how, let alone why, but he finished up on the front row and almost in the middle.

I'm sure you can anticipate what happened on the day of the inspection, every serviceman's worst nightmare when on parade. As we began to present arms, Jenkins dropped his rifle. There is an unspoken saying in the ranks that if anything like that ever happens, pretend to faint, go down and stay down. Nobody had told Jenkins this, so just to make a meal of it he sort of scrabbled around to retrieve it, bashing and clattering as he did so, finally achieving the present position several seconds after the rest of us.

From the safety of the back row, I was trying to stop pissing myself but this pillock had probably done himself a favour by excusing himself from ever having to be on parade again. No self-respecting drill NCO would ever want him around.

I often wondered what happened to Jenkins. I believe the expression was 'his prospects were slight!'

25. The Prison

I pushed a pound note into the sweaty hand of the diminutive, sharp-suited Cypriot manager of *The Prison* disco and turned to my Irish mate, indicating for him to join me in coming through, past the entrance desk.

'Come on Paddy, I've paid for you.'

The short-arse manager, probably some 20 years older but a fair bit smaller and slighter than me, blocked our way.

'Eet's a pound each,' he claimed abruptly.

'No 'eet' isn't,' I argued. 'Eet's feefty pence each before 10 o'clock.'

'Eet *ees* 10 o'clock.' He pointed to the clock on the wall, which read exactly 10 pm. I wasn't finished yet.

'But *they* paid fifty pence.' I pointed out our four mates ahead of us, who were just disappearing round the corner out of sight into the disco.

'But they were 'ere *before* 10 o'clock!' Short-Arse claimed triumphantly, continuing to bar our way.

'Oh, bollocks,' I retorted wittily and pushed past him, urging the hesitant Paddy to follow. What followed, I can still scarcely believe. Short-Arse shouted for help and a big fat bouncer appeared from round the corner. With almost no hesitation and certainly no provocation, I punched the bouncer full on the chin with my fist. Me – I punched a bouncer! I've never, ever hit anyone like that in my life, honestly. The bouncer appeared more surprised than hurt. He was about three times my size and strangely reacted by shouting for more help. A moment of sanity prevailed as I suddenly realised I – or should I say we – were now in big, big trouble.

Paddy and I had just descended into an underground disco called *The Prison* in Limassol, Cyprus. The year was 1969, I was 20 years old and on a three-week detachment to Cyprus. A detachment was a sort of paid holiday in the sun, courtesy of Her Majesty. We had been very heavily warned NOT to step out of line in Cyprus, there were so many different authorities lying in wait, itching for British servicemen like us to step out of line so that they could jump on us. United Nations police, Greek police, Turkish police, Army police, Navy police and of course, our 'friends' I-don't-think, the RAF police somewhere out there, just waiting to jump all over us innocent lads if we were to make exhibitions of ourselves – and here I was, asking for it.

Why had I done it, if it was so out of character? You may already be marking me down as some punchy little yob in uniform, but before sentencing I would like to add, in mitigation, that I had never done anything like this in my life before, or since. I am not a coward but neither am I aggressive or antagonistic. Probably I'm a bit of a pacifist, odd considering I was a serviceman (hey, I was there to service aircraft, not shoot people). I have only had three fights in my life and lost them all, so to say this was 'not like me at all' is a massive understatement.

The real answer as to why I committed this heinous crime lies in drink and money. In the sixties and seventies in Cyprus, one went out socially for a meal, known as a 'kebab' but totally different to the well-known UK fast-food version. This was a full meal, to be enjoyed slowly over several hours. I think from memory there were about five or six different courses: chicken, beef, pork, lamb and more, with lashings of salads and vegetables and a lovely sweet to end with. When it came to drink, for a small outlay you could purchase a decent wine to wash this very pleasant meal down with. However, if this slight charge was firmly declined, as we did, then free wine was supplied with the meal.

I say 'wine' but in truth I am unsure today what it actually was. It was called *Kokinelli*,[4] was almost black, like ink, in appearance and it tasted vile. Being free, of course, we drank it copiously, a new bottle always quickly replacing the empty one. But the awful taste was not the worst thing about Kokinelli, it was the bizarre, brain scrambling effect it had on you that was the most frightening; it must have been very strong. When you were drunk on Kokinelli almost anything could happen and invariably did. I actually had a

---

[4] Kokinelli is locally-produced Cypriot red wine or 'village wine'. Also used for cleaning carburettors and paint stripping. Do not mix with KEO beer. *Source:* Army Rumour Service website.

bit of a reputation in those days as a big drinker who could hold it, courtesy of my father, and was normally known as one who could go on a bit more than most in the drinking stakes. But Kokinelli, well, all bets were off when consuming quantities of that. Needless to say, that night at *The Prison* I had consumed a considerable amount of Kokinelli, and was thus rendered temporarily insane: hence hitting the bouncer.

I hope the latter information has shed some light as to why I, of all people, would react as I did over such a relatively minor matter as an entrance fee. But strike the behaviour-enforcer I did, and if there's any good news it's that fortunately the possible consequences of my actions quickly came home to me like a sledgehammer. So, in truly heroic style, I turned and ran back to the bottom of the steps, intending to get up the steps and out of the place as soon as possible. But in my haste I had forgotten Paddy, a true friend and ally in every sense of the word.

Looking back down the narrow passageway, Paddy was retreating steadily with his back to me, head down but flailing right and left punches like Joe Frazier. Advancing slowly on him was not Mohammed Ali but a small crowd of nasty looking bouncers, leering and shouting obscenities at us. As Paddy arrived at the bottom of the steps I lashed out with him in a final flurry at the opposition. I vaguely remember there were some minor contacts on both sides, then we turned, leapt up the stone steps and out into the night, plunging down many narrow streets as fast as we could before, exhausted, we came to a small square.

A taxi obligingly came round the corner and we dived into it, gasping the name of our camp, eighteen miles away. As we sped away, Paddy and I cowered low on the seats until we eventually cleared the town and were taken back to the safety of Royal Air Force Station, Akrotiri.

But that is not quite the end of the story.

Back at the camp, in our block, which was relatively quiet and still, I went off for a bath to unwind and relax. Paddy went straight to sleep, fortunately with no interrogation of me as to the reason for my insane behaviour. As I lay in the bath, strange smelly brown objects appeared in the bath with me, as if I had no control of my bowels. It must have been some nervous reaction after a shock to the system.

In the morning I felt better and apparently restored to relative sanity I felt ready to discuss the previous night's escapades. Before I could get dressed someone in our room pointed out that I had some strange marks on my chest. I went to the mirror and held up my arms. In a beautifully symmetrical line from one side of my torso to the other were the perfect marks of the links of a bicycle chain in weals and bruises.

I could just about dimly recall something whirling around in the dim lighting of The Prison as I tried to extricate Paddy from his brave, Alamo-like stance as he took on all comers. Paddy couldn't recall any details from the night before but that wasn't unusual in his case. Paddy didn't need Kokinelli to act bizarrely, it was built into his DNA, but he was a good bloke to have on your side in times of trouble – or stupidity in my case. I was extremely lucky to get away with only a sore chest and some heavy mickey-taking. I never went back to *The Prison,* for obvious reasons and grew to respect and fear Kokinelli as a very dangerous substance which could ruin a reputation. I wonder if they still serve it: if so it should have a government health warning!

26. Steve and The Big Apple

Val was fed up with waiting for Steve to ask her to marry him. He, in turn, had no intention of doing so, at least not for a good while, and was casting envious glances at our Saturday night antics while he was at the pictures with Val. Still, he did have the bonus that they slept together regularly in her bed while we were out desperately searching and mostly failing to do likewise, before we all joined up together on Sunday morning to play football and then together we all enjoyed our Sunday nights out again.

Val, who was a bright, lively girl, then went and got herself a job as a hotel receptionist in Bermuda, which gave Steve the green light to make up for lost time on Saturday nights – which he did with great gusto (that's one way of putting it). Now as luck would have it, our 'jolly' run to Singapore via Malta and Gan,[5] a gorgeous little island in the Maldives, had just been changed.

You'll never guess where the NAVEX was changed to? Yes, you've got it from previous chapters – Bermuda. It was usually a straight run to Bermuda over the Atlantic, then one or two nights at *The Castle Harbour Hotel,* which overlooked the bay at Hamilton, the Bermudan capital. After Bermuda there was a one-night stopover at Larges, the USAF base in the Azores, where you were guaranteed a great night out as guests of the Americans.

Steve and Val had not finished with each other, they were still in touch, so opportunity knocked. At first glance I thought I could have done better out of the deal but then I didn't have a fiancée in Bermuda. Neither did Steve, actually, but that's what he told the Wing Commander when he asked permission to go out on a flight to Bermuda, stay one week and catch the next flight back a week later. Steve had a good, well-deserved reputation as a sound NCO, he was well thought of and permission was granted. I was picked to

---

[5] *From Port T to RAF Gan*, published by Woodfield, traces the history of this remote outpost of Empire in the Maldives from before the First World War to the closure of the RAF base in the 1970s.

be on the flight out with him but destined only to spend one night with he and Val in Bermuda before flying on to the Azores.

But – ABC – *All Bin Changed* meant that all of a sudden things got better ... for me anyway. We heard that we were to go on from Bermuda to... wait for it ... New York, carrying some spares for an aircraft that had had a small fire a few days earlier at La Guardia airport. Whoopee! The prospect of leaving my best mate in Bermuda for an idyllic week softened at the thought of a day and night experiencing the delights of The Big Apple.

The great day dawned and we set off on our noisy, vibrating, uncomfortable fourteen-hour journey in a plane designed to carry freight, not people but buoyed by thoughts of excitement ahead.

Normally it's aircrew who get the perks and the groundcrew who see the shittier side of aircraft life, to put it bluntly, but picture this... We were met at the tiny Bermuda airport by two lovely tanned young women, as Val had thoughtfully brought her flatmate Sally (who didn't look flat to me, very nicely rounded!) and they had come along on their little mopeds to collect us. How thoughtful! The hardly-believing-but-envious-looks we got from the flight crew were fantastic as we jumped on the back of the bikes, the girls promising to the captain and crew to deliver me back first thing in the morning to travel on to New York. Doesn't get much better than that, now does it?

Back at the girls' flat, Steve and I quickly showered, changed and we all walked up to the Police club to celebrate our arrival. We settled in the comfortable lounge of the police club and got down to some serious drinking, which we seemed in the right place to enjoy. Of course, I immediately set about chatting up Val's attractive flat mate but quickly became disillusioned about the prospect of any romance as she seemed to be in a serious relationship. Apparently, he was due in town next week, so I resolved just to enjoy her company for the evening (*Mental note:* must try not to get amorous later when alcohol kicks in seriously. *Further mental note:* who are you trying to kid?).

Meanwhile Steve and Val were busily re-kindling their relationship but I had forgotten that their relationship could be volatile and, after a few drinks, the temperature began to rise. Steve was dutifully taken to task for his poor communication skills (I could have shed some light on the reason but wisely kept my mouth shut). Eventually it was becoming heated – the path of true love? – so Sally and I decided to give them some space and went for a walk, via one or two other bars. She was a very pretty girl but made it perfectly plain that there was nothing doing. What a pity but never mind, Johnny Mac, there was plenty more action to happen on the trip...

By the time we arrived back later, it was obvious from the strewn discarded clothes, closed bedroom door and noises from the inside that some serious making-up was going on. Sally made up my bed on the settee and gave me a consoling platonic peck on the cheek before retiring herself to her bedroom with a firm 'goodnight, Mac'. There were no chinks of light to give me any naughty ideas and, anyway, after the long flight I fell into a deep sleep.

I woke in the middle of the night, bursting for a wee and headed off, naked, down the passage to the bathroom. As I opened the door to come out, with the light still on, I met Val, also stark naked, who didn't bat an eyelid or anything else. I think she was still a bit tipsy, Val liked a drink. Ever the gentleman, when I gallantly stepped back to allow her in she smiled sweetly and said, 'Thanks, Mac', as if it was the most natural thing in the world. Continuing to nakedly face her (it seemed rude to turn my back) as if in some kind of medieval dance, we seemed to almost 'size each other up' as we changed places.

From my perspective the exchange was very pleasant, I hadn't really noticed before that Val was beautifully and generously built, with everything seemingly perfectly in place. Just as nature began to rush to take its course, the bathroom door gently closed against my willy (with me outside!); I thought it best to return to my lonely settee, keeping up the gallantry, if nothing much else, by now. Several minutes later, I heard doors opening and closing, and then quiet. Nothing was said in the morning. I stored it up in my mind to perhaps mention to Steve at a later date but I never did.

If our mode of arrival caused the aircrew some raised eyebrows, so did my departure. I bade a teeth-gritted farewell to Steve (lucky bastard), Val gave me a hug and a peck, with no indication of having remembered anything – did I dream it? No, I remembered the lovely curves of her boobs and bum too well and my surging reaction to them). Sally, bless her, primed by Steve, gave me a hug and ever-so-slightly lingering kiss to wind up the aircrew, who were observing closely. Hey, wasn't it they who were supposed to get all the perks?

Off we flew, leaving the idyllic island of Bermuda behind and flying north on a relatively short flight to New York. One of the aircrew was a flight sergeant who was known as 'Shipley Pete' and was a proud Yorkshireman with a great sense of humour, hailing from Shipley (pronounced *Shipleh*) which, according to him, was the centre of the universe. Pete used to play in our station football team but, being aircrew, he was sometimes away. One miserable, cold, wet, winter Wednesday we were told he was away. When we asked where we were told 'Hawaii' – that went down well, as you could imagine. The next week Pete bowled into the changing rooms and someone asked him what Hawaii had been like. He paused, looked up, as if for divine inspiration and uttered the immortal words.

'Well... It were *almost* as good as Shipleh on a Friday night.'

Wow – it must have been *really* good then, we all agreed.

Our flight to New York landed in mid-afternoon and I thought I had really arrived as we checked into the luxurious Lexington Hotel on Lexington Avenue in Manhattan. It all seemed so far from what and where I had come from, a boy from the Midlands, to be suddenly deposited in the centre of one of the world's most exciting cities. How lucky was I, at nineteen, to experience this? Two things stuck in my mind afterwards about the trip. The first was going up the Empire State Building, at the time the highest man-made monument in the world. I recall the skyscraper lift being so fast it took your breath away and on getting to the observation tower, the highest public area allowed, stepping out onto the airy platform with its chest high railings was quite an experience. I looked out to see the tops of various other skyscrapers that were not as high as we were but then I looked down... and down and down, until I realised from the size of the minute cars in the tiny street just how very, very high we were. It was quite a shock to realise that man had built this himself. How was it possible? I imagined helping in the construction and remembered those fabulous photos of construction workers sitting on girders thousands of feet in the air as they took their meal breaks – unbelievable!

Safely back down to earth, Pete and I continued our stroll around Manhattan. We saw the famous Times Square and marvelled at Macy's and Bloomingdales from the outside. We stopped in a couple of bars for a drink where we sat on high stools at the bar, trying to look like Americans, eventually taking a last stroll around the now deserted streets of Manhattan before turning in.

As we were passing a large, darkened department store, from the shadows of the doorway out stepped Diana Ross. Well, if it wasn't actually my Motown idol, then in my innocent young mind, she came pretty close. This girl was black, petite, beautifully dressed and very, very pretty. She came over towards us, stopping a few feet away. 'Diana' tilted her head to one side, smiled and said sweetly 'Hi, there – are you guys looking for a girl?' She pronounced girl as *gurrrl*, rolling her r's (all jokes welcome) in a very sexy way. To put it mildly, I was thunderstruck and unable to speak. I just could not believe that this beautiful creature was a member of the oldest profession. All the prostitutes I had seen in places like Malta were haggard, ugly, world-weary and cynical. They were not like this. But before anything could happen, 'Uncle Pete' firmly took control of the situation.

'No ta, dook,' he replied in broad Yorkshire, helpfully adding 'Don't think LOA could stand it,' before gently leading me away.

LOA, as reported elsewhere, stood for Local Overseas Allowance, a laid-down daily amount of subsistence varying according to where one was in the world. It had not occurred to me to link the two but obviously Pete had. To tell the truth, despite being in the services, I had never been anywhere near a prostitute, apart from being in bars where they were operating but I had definitely never seen anything like Diana before – or since as it happens.

Pete guided me safely back to the hotel and back to the UK the following day. As usual he enthralled the rest of the football team in the dressing room the following week with tales of our trip.

Recounted by a raconteur and member of our aircrew like Pete, who had observed – with deep respect – Sally, me and the moped disappearing for the night, to re-emerge the next day, Pete enhanced my reputation with the lads considerably as I modestly allowed them to fantasise about what had happened.

Nothing, as you know, but you don't want to let the facts spoil a good story, now do you?

It had hurt leaving my best mate in paradise but to go on to New York and meet Diana made up for it. I thought she was – Supreme!

Sorry, couldn't resist it!

27. The Mecca Run

Quite how we devised 'The Mecca Run' I don't recall. It wasn't exactly calculated and executed like a military manoeuvre such as The Dam Busters raid but it had a sort of plan to it. My twenty-first birthday was coming up on Saturday 5th March 1970 and we decided to celebrate it with a big night out. There had been a few dummy runs in various formats but this was the first real beginning, middle and end plan to a particular night that we had tried to follow ... and this is how the evening went.

It began early, with teatime food at 4 pm, followed by showers or baths, then, dressed to kill in suits, shirts and ties, and well doused in Brut aftershave, we had to be out to catch the 6 pm bus off the camp. This lumbered down into the village and we just had time for one pint in our local, *The Railway Inn* before the 6:30 Portsmouth train arrived. The plan was not to travel right into the city centre and the ultimate bright lights but to get off at Fratton. Fratton Park was the home ground of Portsmouth FC, where we spent many long hours, mainly fruitlessly, urging the useless buggers on. This time it was a serious journey, however, as we were to embark on a major pub-crawl, steadily working our way into the centre of Pompey and our goal – the Mecca Dance Hall!

I seem to remember there were easily twelve, if not more, pubs on the way. The rule was only one pint in each, so if we kept up a steady pace, we would arrive at the Mecca sometime before 10 pm. We needed to be there before ten because they would not let you in after that (drinking laws and opening hours were very different then). It was to prevent drunks getting in, enough said, so we had to be on our best behaviour as we approached the doors. Not too easy with a dozen pints sloshing around inside you, but we usually managed it. Very few were not allowed in because they couldn't stand up straight or speak coherently (we practiced it – you had to say 'Chichester' without slurring it – difficult if you were really pissed).

The Mecca itself was the local big gaudy dance hall, there's one in every city under various names; it was the same place where we were initially and frighteningly told that if you couldn't pick up a young woman there, you might as well shoot yourself. The problem was that the quality of available young women was highly dubious: if you wanted sparkling wit, decent chat and a bit of fun, you had probably gone to the wrong place. I'm not saying that some weren't pretty but when you live in an all-male environment like the armed forces all week, almost anything in a skirt looks attractive on a Saturday night, especially with a dozen pints inside you. Of course, the decent ones had almost always been snapped up by eagle-eyed locals by ten but hey, we didn't care too much, we weren't overly choosy, the last thing we were looking for at that stage of our lives was a wife.

I recall being very embarrassed about one unsavoury incident from my own twenty-first recounted at lunch the next day in the mess. My drinks had been spiked early on, so my memory was much impaired, but I was assured it happened. Someone said 'My favourite bit last night was the Zulu Warrior with the old dear's hat and the beer' Everyone except me fell about laughing. A 'Zulu Warrior' was a full male strip, with tribal chanting and rhythmical clapping, as one central figure, hamming it up to the beat, stripped his clothes off as erotically as possible until totally naked. He would then be drenched as everyone's drink was thrown at him, amid huge cheers and applause. Needless to say, it was usually an in-house affair, conducted in Naafis, military bars and clubs, with largely male audiences, mainly but not always abroad, usually done to lighten the boredom.

'Who did the Zulu Warrior?' I heard myself say.

Disbelieving eyes turned on me.

'You mean you don't remember, Mac? God, it was so funny when you whipped off your shreds (pants) and threw them at the old lady sitting in the corner. They landed on her head and then you climbed onto the bench seat beside her, waving your willy at her and everyone in the bar!'

I wanted to disbelieve them but somehow I knew they weren't lying. There was no need. Normally I remembered most of what happened on boozy nights; as much as the next man, anyway.

But there was more. The poor old dear was wearing a hat with a brim and my overflowing beer spilled onto it, whereupon it ran round the brim and leaked from the little holes on either side, much to everyone in the pub's amusement. I was assured the old lady loved it and apparently I insisted on buying her a drink before we left as she was such a good sport.

Did I really do that? Not buying the drink, the Zulu warrior? Yes, I was convinced by everyone that I did, so I must have done.

There was another major incident that night – Tim's story. As the post-mortems began to subside, one of my best mates confided in me that he had met a girl the previous night and had arranged to go out with her that night (Sunday) but wasn't going to go. When I asked why not, Tim stated that he was so drunk he couldn't remember what she looked like, only when and where to meet her and her name – Lorna. I urged him to go but he was very dubious; his view was that any girl who would look at him seriously if he was that drunk couldn't be up to much.

The normal plan on Sunday nights was a 15-mile trip in the other direction to Portsmouth into West Sussex and to a very smart club called the Bali-Hai in Pagham, an upmarket suburb of Bognor Regis. The Bali-Hai[6] had a dress code and you took a girl there on a quiet weekday night if you wanted to impress her, or went on a Sunday with the lads, when there was a good disco and sometimes some decent spare young women about. I persuaded Tim to give it a go and his last words before he left to meet her were, 'You probably won't see me later, but if she's half-decent, I might bring her there.'

About two hours later I was at the bar waiting to be served, when a voice in my ear said. 'Hey, Mac, come and look at this.' I went over to the table where four of our mates were eagerly clustered round a very pretty blonde girl in a short mini-skirt – Lorna! Everything was just where it should be, in spades, and she had a bubbly funny way about her: she looked a bit like the blonde one in ABBA. We all fancied her like mad and were envious of Tim,

---

[6] The Bali-Hai plus other well-known South Coast venues of the 60s and the musicians who played at them is told in *The South Coast Beat Scene of the 1960s* by BBC broadcaster Mike Read, published by Woodfield in 2001.

who couldn't believe his luck. We had to be quickly sworn to secrecy as Tim had told her that he worked for IBM, one of our favourite fibs. We never admitted that we were serving in Her Majesty's armed forces, although in those days of long hair it wasn't too difficult to work out. Tim and Lorna's relationship went from strength to strength and eventually they became engaged. Tim asked me to be his best man, as we were good mates and I had been so instrumental in bringing them together.

They were married a year later and Tim was almost immediately posted to Gibraltar with Lorna, shortly after I had left the RAF. When Tim followed me, a year later, he also went into selling, joined the same company as me and my father and eventually went to work for Dad. He didn't stay long, moved on to his elder brother's company and went with Lorna to live in Stockholm as European Sales Manager.

We lost touch eventually and I heard they had split up; they didn't have children. About twelve years later, I found myself working in Lorna's home town and dropped by to see her parents, who I always got on with. They told me where she worked and I popped in to see her. The years had not been unkind, her dazzling blue eyes and blonde hair were still exciting and as I was staying in a hotel that night in the area, I asked her out to dinner with me. Lorna came, although she mentioned she was in a relationship with a married man.

I had always fancied her (did I mention that?) but I don't think she quite believed me when I told her my marriage was on the rocks (which was true) and that I was 'available'. At the end of the meal I kissed her gently and suggested we went back to my room but she turned me down. I didn't press her or try to change her mind but when I rang her the next day I asked if we could see each other next time I was 'in town'. She said she'd like that. As it happened, I wasn't down that way again for a good while, then my job changed, so there was little chance. I left it like that. It was probably for the best, but she was a cracker. I bet she still is!

The Mecca Run, originating on my twenty-first birthday on March 5th 1970 became the standard form of celebration from then on, and we did many Mecca Runs during the next couple of years, and great fun they always were – but mine was the first!

28. Hold the Line Please, Caller...

One of the more engaging acts of the authorities who ran the RAF station I worked on was to provide a monthly dance/disco in the NAAFI for we singlies. On a camp of several thousand personnel, almost exclusively male, this would have been useless without women, so the organisers of these events saw fit to target various women's establishments in the area, such as hospitals, nurses homes, teacher training colleges and telephone exchanges, offering to provide free transport in the form of a bus to and from the venue, plus other inducements. For weeks and months afterwards, and occasionally even longer, we would all be going out with nurses, students or, as in this case, telephonists! One or two of these relationships even ended in marriage...

They were a rum lot, the telephonists, just like us they had their own camaraderie and exclusive sense of humour. They were based in nearby Chichester, a lovely old West Sussex town, eight miles away from our camp. One of their favourite tricks was listening in to people's phone calls and alerting each other to anything of interest, so they could all eavesdrop at the same time. A famous member of one of the world's major pop groups, still going today, has always had a big house on the South Coast and calls to and from his house were a rich source of entertainment.

One electric weekend in early 1970 the whole telephone exchange all listened avidly when a leading singer and actress in a famous West End show rang the house to inform the lead singer of the group that she was pregnant by him and what were his intentions? For some reason, he was dubious about his involvement and told her so in so many words, inferring there might be other parties involved. At this she went ballistic, her thrust being that to him this might be the swinging sixties but 'putting it about' was definitely not something she practised. I'm sure neither realised that their blistering row was being listened to by practically the whole telephone exchange, but it was!

It was into this world I blissfully wandered unaware, by dating a petite, attractive, dark-haired telephonist called Jill, after we had met at our monthly disco. She was quite staid really, still living with her parents, and kept me, as best she could, at arm's length when we were alone. We went out for a couple of months but I felt we were not really going anywhere and I was thinking of ending it when an unfortunate incident occurred. Late one weekday night we were returning to Chichester from Bognor Regis from the Bali Hai.

I had had more than the legal limit to drink but was not drunk and we took the longer, quieter, back way home, down a windy country road. I really don't remember exactly what happened. I believe I swerved to miss a rabbit or something, clipped the foot high grass verge at the side of the road and rolled my Triumph Herald pride-and-joy over, coming to rest upside-down on a barbed wire fence. I think I was temporarily knocked out. I came to on the grass verge and could hear Jill crying. For a minute I couldn't work out where she was, until I found her in the cornfield over the fence. She had some nasty scratches on her legs, as I did on my left arm. I still have the scars, but otherwise we were mercifully unharmed.

However, there was blood everywhere and we needed help. A passing couple in a sports car somehow transported us to a nearby cottage hospital but would accept nothing apart from our gratitude (I'm sure we left a lot of blood on their lovely car). As they had no emergency services, the cottage hospital got us transferred by ambulance to the big hospital in Chichester (I had a few nursing friends there) where, after treatment, I was allowed home, but Jill had to be kept in overnight.

I was duly breathalysed and passed, fortunately, but then a really amazing thing happened. I glanced at the hospital notes, which we had filled in separately when we were first treated. I was twenty-one and had told Jill I was twenty-four, the same age she had told me she was. Imagine my surprise to see from her forms that she was actually twenty-nine! Jill was released the next day and I went to see her at home with flowers. All seemed ok but I felt awful that I had decided to end it; now the timing was all wrong, so I told her I would 'ring her next week' to arrange another date.

Steve, my lifelong mate, came to the hospital, took me back to the camp and then, the next day, back to the scene of the accident.

His face was one of sheer disbelief at how we had walked away virtually unscathed when the car looked so bad. With difficulty we managed to tow it back to the camp, where repairs to the Herald took several months and feature in another story (Lawbreaking).

The following week, he and I were out on the razz as usual, ending up in another of our haunts, a club called 'The Kontiki' on Hayling Island, a regular stamping ground of ours, where we spotted two likely-looking lovelies standing chatting near the edge of the dance floor. Our gentlemen's agreement meant that we took it in turns to go for the best looking one – it was his turn and she was a cracker. Just to be sure I hadn't forgotten it was his turn, Steve stood on my foot and elbowed me in the guts before setting off to ask the pretty one to dance, leaving me temporarily winded and a couple of paces behind.

By the time I got there, 'mine' was talking to two other blokes. Not to be outdone, I tapped her politely on the shoulder and she swung round. I could see she was a little older and not so stunning as Steve's, but still relatively gorgeous. She said she was sorry but no, and turned back to continue her conversation. When you are out there on a regular basis on the pick-up, with a mate who you know well, such situations occur often. I wasn't too worried, settling back to wait and see how Steve fared. Imagine my surprise when suddenly a sweet-smelling vision appeared at my elbow.

'I'm sorry about that, someone asked me something and I had to reply but if the offer still stands, I'd love to dance with you'. While dancing, she told me that her name was Raquel, the two were sisters and she was the elder. We ended up taking the girls home. Steve dropped me off to say goodnight to Raquel at her flat, while he took the sister back to the parents, with whom she still lived. In her porchway, Raquel and I had a little kiss and cuddle and we got on really well. She had an impish sense of humour and a twinkle in her eye that I liked. I asked to see her again, she said yes and we agreed to go out in a few days time, if Steve would lend me his car.

My good mate said ok on the spot when he came to pick me up and I took Raquel to a quiet club I knew – yes, my old stamping ground for such occasions, the Bali-Hai at Bognor. Looking back, I remember it got a bit steamy on the dance floor but I put that down to my new aftershave. When we got back to her flat, Raquel invited me in for coffee, as long as I promised to be quiet. Her landlady, who lived downstairs, did not approve of her entertaining late at night. I agreed, we crept in and she disappeared. I sat quietly on the settee, obediently waiting and fully expecting coffee. I was not used to being invited in by mature women with their own flats, most of my affairs were with giggly girls in the backs of cars who fought me gently for control of their knickers.

Aren't women strange? It doesn't happen often in life but sometimes – well you just strike lucky! To my utter amazement Raquel appeared at the doorway in a skimpy negligee and put one finger to her lips suggesting silence and beckoning with the other hand. I did not need any further encouragement and we slipped into her bedroom. She whispered that I couldn't stay the night. I nodded dumbly, unable to speak but managing everything else required and all my birthdays came at once – pretty quickly, as I recall.

Raquel was mature and experienced in ways I wasn't. She had been married previously, she had explained, but was now separated and living alone. Intense 'blow-your-socks-off' sexual encounters of this kind were few and far between, so it was stupid not to take full advantage, and I did! She whispered that she had felt so up-for-it that it would have happened on the dance floor if there hadn't been a crowd. I remember thinking 'Wow! What have I got here?'

Later, after quietly and dizzily descending the stairs on the way out, at her door we realised we hadn't made any further plans to see each other. She told me to ring her in the morning at work. This sexual bombshell then told me where she worked, the well-known company's number was in the phone book.

"Just ask the switchboard for Raquel De La Plante" she said.

'Very exotic,' I thought.

After regaling Steve with my sexploits (we shared everything) he pointed out some bites and scratches on me. The next morning, I went to the phone box to ring Raquel. As usual on the camp there was no phone book, so I rang Directory Enquiries. A familiar voice answered, saying 'Directory Enquiries' and I asked for the number.

'Is that you, John?' asked the voice. 'How are you? Do you want to ring me back here after your call and we can have a chat? Your number is Cosham 625744, by the way'.

It was Jill, of course, so I was now in a predicament. I thanked her but replaced the receiver and tried to get the dialling tone back. I couldn't and eventually a different female voice said, 'Are you having trouble caller? What number are you ringing?' Without thinking, I told her the number, was put through immediately and asked for Raquel. After a second, a deep sexy voice answered and I told her it was me.

'Hello Blossom – and how are we today?' We went through thirty minutes of steamy conversation, even comparing physically chafed 'bits', before eventually agreeing to do it all again on Friday night.

I opened the door of the phone box to leave, then suddenly guiltily remembered Jill. I phoned Directory Enquiries and we chatted uneasily for several minutes before she said, 'Well, John, are we going to see each other again? How about Friday?'

I said I couldn't on Friday, as I was on nights (the standard excuse). We left it that I would ring her the following week (which I didn't). I walked back thoughtfully to tell Steve, nursing a warm glow and those few sore bits Raquel and I had discussed.

Raquel and I enjoyed another high-octane Friday night, and then Sunday until the following week, when I actually *was* on nights. During the evening I went to the Sailing Club, a very sociable place on our island, for a liquid meal break. Down the other end of the bar I spotted another girl from the telephonists group called Dee, who was seeing another airman who I vaguely knew. The two were chatting together. Our eyes met along the bar and she seemed to choke on her drink. She laughed and said something to her boyfriend and he laughed too. I thought it was a bit strange but took no notice. After a few minutes I saw Dee get up, heading, I presumed, for the loo. She had to pass me on the way and she stopped and gave me a huge saucy wink.

'Hey, Blossom!' She laughed. 'Sounded a great night that, John! How's your sore bits, then? Doin' anything Friday night?'

I couldn't believe it. Had they done me? Surely not me? What could I say?

'You... bastards!' I mumbled, helplessly.

They had done me – and I just didn't see it coming. And I should have. After all, I had been warned that they listened in.

I should add that while we were enamoured with one of these lovely girls it was brilliant for telephoning anyone like your Mum or family for free. You just phoned up the exchange and said 'Is so and so in?' and if they weren't they'd say 'No, but xxxx is, do you want to speak to her?' Whoever you spoke to would then connect you to almost anywhere for nothing, for as long as you wanted. They were very generous and full of fun ... if you played it their way!

Raquel and me? Our all-too-brief relationship was short, sharp, glorious and very passionate. But what I didn't know at that time was that she had only lately separated from her very-nasty-piece-of-work husband. She had moved into her flat alone and was beginning to enjoy life again by going out socially with her lovely sister – cue John! I was separately warned, through football contacts who I played with (her husband was a very good, well-known local footballer), not to mess with him or what he considered his. He had apparently been 'inside' for several unpleasant incidents involving people who had got on the wrong side of him. I didn't want to be another!

After three passion-filled weeks, she rang me to say she was going back to him, that she was sorry but thanks for some lovely times we'd had. At that time, newly-armed with the above information about her nutter of a husband, I was going through a 'head versus heart' mental debate (well, head versus willy, to be more precise), so it was something of a relief when the whole thing was taken from my hands anyway.

Raquel and I parted on great terms with lovely memories. It's not often your wildest dreams come true but Raquel certainly made mine do just that – and the GPO girls all had a good laugh at my expense – so everyone was happy!

29. Gordon's Wedding Weekend

Gordon was a mysterious bugger; you never knew what he was up to. He was 'one of us' but wasn't as well, if you know what I mean. He came out socially with us sometimes, occasionally picking up women, occasionally getting drunk, but not often, as he was also away a lot. He was a good goalkeeper, we all thought he could have made it professionally, but he claimed his ankles had been too weak as he grew up. At one point he went off to the RAF Hospital for several months to have an operation on his leg, or something but on his return, and after several mysterious long weekends away, we were all astounded when he asked a small circle of us, his closest mates, if we wanted to come to a wedding: his!

It transpired that he had become very friendly with a nurse at the hospital and had been secretly seeing her on those weekends when he was away, which was often with Gordon. It transpired that his bride-to-be, Meryl (great name) came from a village up on the Norfolk coast. That, of course, was where the wedding was to be, a couple of months hence. As it turned out, one of our younger lads, Lee, who we also played football with and was loosely on the edge of our 'gang', came from not many miles away from Meryl's village, where the intended nuptials were to be held.

So we rigged Lee an invitation from Gordon, that way we could all stay at Lee's parents' house for the weekend, five of us! After a lengthy discussion regarding cars it was decided, rather against my will, for reasons I will explain, that we take my car, an old Vauxhall Victor (known as VV), on the grounds that it was the biggest and could therefore accommodate us all best.

The problem was that it was nearing its great final journey, not upwards to the sky but down the road to the breakers yard. A good car in its day but those days and years were definitely far behind it and VV was beginning to burn a little too much oil for comfort!

Still, that was our decision and we stuck to it.

At the time I was going out with a rather attractive willowy blond called Jo (there are lurid other stories about her elsewhere in this book) from teachers training college in Bognor. She was going home to Watford for the holidays, so I gallantly offered her a lift, as we were going her way, it seemed churlish not to.

So off we all set one Friday lunchtime, Jo sandwiched in the back between two of my lusty mates, who enjoyed that stage of the journey, they told me later. After dropping off my beloved, with unreliable promises from me to communicate regularly (see elsewhere for details) we pressed on all the way up to East Anglia, never a short, easy journey. Sure enough, VV was beginning to emit a trail of blue smoke as we arrived at our destination.

Lee, our host, then revealed that his Dad was the local copper, a real Mr Plod village policeman, with a round ruddy face and a lovely tubby wife to match. They made us very welcome, gave us a square meal and, after a few beers at the local, we all slept somehow in Mark's sister's bedroom. I'm not sure where she was for the weekend. The highlight of the evening, I remember, was us all taking turns to try on Lee's sister's long blonde wig, which sat on a polystyrene head on her dressing table. As we were in the forces, we had never seen each other with long hair, so it was fantastically funny for us, no doubt aided by the alcohol, to each look like one of the Rolling Stones just for once in our lives.

The big day arrived and we took it in turns to ponce ourselves up for the event, the bathroom fully occupied for hours. Scrubbed up, shaved and in our suits, we looked very presentable and set off for the half-hour journey to the village and its church. We were in very good time of course, enough to have a good session in the local pub, as all good mates do prior to the wedding.

Before long, two smart bright lovelies joined us, who turned out to be Gordon's sisters. They were great fun and delighted in playing *match the face* to the stories they had heard about us from their brother. It appeared that Gordon had discussed us all at great length when he was home at weekends and there were one or two embarrassed faces to questions like, 'Did you *really* do a full strip in the pub on your twenty-first party, Mac?'

By the time we had to move the few hundred yards along the High Street to the little church, everyone was getting along fine, other family members and friends had joined us, and the atmosphere was warm and friendly. At that stage about six pints each had been consumed, but that was par for the course, we could handle that without making exhibitions of ourselves in those days.

Because Gordon was such a secretive sod, we were all curious to see Meryl, as we hadn't even seen a picture. We later found out that she was two months pregnant, although at that stage no-one knew or noticed. Apart from ascertaining that she was a redhead and about five feet five, her veil covered her face as she came down the aisle so we had to wait a bit longer. The service was nice. As an ex-choirboy I had attended many weddings in my time and appreciated such events. We spilled out into the churchyard and in turn Gordon introduced us to his new bride. She was quiet and shy but seemed very nice and polite. Looking back, it must have been quite an ordeal for the poor girl, meeting five of us for the first time all at once.

We thirstily burst into the big lounge bar of a small hotel down the road, which had been reserved for the reception. After stopping for an hour or so for the wedding, the beer then flowed well, so during the next few hours of the afternoon another six pints went down as the very informal buffet-style reception worked well and we all made new friends. At one stage, Gordon was enjoying himself so much he called on each of us to make a short speech, and we all duly tried to embarrass him without getting too coarse.

Everything appeared to go down well and eventually we got some tin cans and anything that made a noise and tied them to Gordon's car bumper. Imagine our surprise when Gordon and Meryl came out of the Hotel, got into his uncle's (loaned) car and drove off, laughing and waving, to go on their honeymoon. His uncle had to untie the cans and drive Gordon's car away! It was about six o'clock by that time.

A post mortem and a *where shall we go from here* meeting was held as we finished our drinks in the bar. Everyone except Dave, our quiet-but-blunt Mancunian amigo, had offered reasonably positive impressions re Meryl, so his opinion was sought.

After taking a long swallow and thinking for a minute, he frowned and came out with his delightful homespun observation.

'She's gorra spotty clock!'

A somewhat harsh assessment but that was Dave for you.

Decisions made, we headed off to Great Yarmouth for a Saturday night out. By this time, the twelve pints we had each consumed meant that everything was hilarious as we noisily moved from pub to pub along the front. Despite a few half-hearted attempts to chat up loose women (there didn't seem to be many about, perhaps word had got round) and annoying a few locals with our noisy banter, the evening proved fairly uneventful and, after closing time at eleven, it was time to head back to our adopted village home.

Yes, it had been another six-pint session and I am reluctant to admit that I took the wheel without thinking too much about it, heading back out of town. In what seemed like a matter of several minutes, my colleagues fell asleep one-by-one and I was left alone awake, charged with the important responsibility of getting my mates safely back. I can still remember the quiet lanes, not getting lost as the signposts were clear, and we were soon back at Lee's parents. Yes, I know, I had drunk eighteen pints during a long day, but on that occasion I can remember most of it, even driving back in a fairly careful and restrained manner.

'Oh, are we back already? I'm knackered, I'm going to bed' was the sum of the appreciative comments I got.

After a huge breakfast the next morning from Lee's lovely Mum and Dad and our profuse thanks to them, we piled back into VV for the six hour journey back. We hadn't gone too far before she began to heat up and the blue smoke from our exhaust began to intensify. It became a matter of some concern whether we would actually make our destination but a combination of gentle 40 mph driving and a lot – and I mean a lot – of engine oil, we limped on until we realised that we were probably going to make it.

The last twenty miles were excruciatingly embarrassing, you couldn't see anything behind us but smoke and everyone was complaining because the air was blue in the car as well. But make it we did, just, although I really don't think VV would have gone much further. It proved to be VV's last journey, ending with the ignominy of her being towed down the A27 to one of my many second homes, Yates's cars breakers yard. Still, she had got us all there and back, bless her, plus a good day and night out, so fond memories all round of a great old car and a great weekend.

30. Laurel and Hardy

Steve was a better footballer than me but he always encouraged me, eventually inviting me to play with him for a civilian team from nearby Haying Island on Sundays. They were a rough but friendly lot and there were invariably punch-ups in the games we played in, depending on the time of day we kicked off. If it was a morning game, they were usually hung-over from the night before, as we were often, but we were fitter and handled it better, although normally, as the game went on, they got better.

Sunday afternoon games, however, were a complete lottery. The civvy lads were mostly pissed from the hard-drinking two hours allowed for Lord's Day pub drinking in those days. We would start off playing like Brazil for about fifteen minutes, scoring terrific goals and looking as if we would murder the opposition but it couldn't and didn't last. Soon they were being sick at the side of the pitch, then we were short-handed and conceded goals easily. We would lose games 6-4, or 5-3, much to my and Steve's disgust but the games were never dull, being always full of fights and goals.

Soon after we started playing for them, a couple of figures began to appear regularly on the touchline. Two young women, good friends, watched our games: one a nice ,robust blonde, fairly broad in the beam and the other completely the opposite, very slim, petite and dark but both girls were very pretty. These two contrasting lovelies we nicknamed *Laurel and Hardy* for obvious reasons. We knew one of them was directly related to at least one of the mafia-type lads in our team, with their long hair and mutton-chop sideboards so we were surprised and flattered when in the changing rooms our team-mates told us that we were the interest that brought the girls to the touchline. It transpired that my 'fan' appeared to be the heftier one and Steve's admirer the skinny one. We didn't mind; funnily enough, that suited us.

We took them out a few times and they were great fun to be around. It was mine who was related to a few characters in the team. Her name was Paula and her brother Gordon played left back to my right back. Paula's elder sister Babs was married to our centre half and captain Willy, a fearsome sight on the field. Willy did not take prisoners. He was a great bloke to have on your side, much better than having to play against him. When his wife Babs pulled me into the pantry for a swift cuddle and grope at their party, I was convulsed with fear about what Willy would do to me if he caught us. I had seen what he did to opponents on the football field when he lost his temper, but I survived. I found out afterwards he was down the garden with his neighbour's wife at the time.

Steve's extremely slim partner was called Jill. She was quite wealthy in comparison to Paula and lived in a big posh house near the seafront on Hayling Island. This island near Havant and Portsmouth had lots of rental homes and holiday camps and was our second home for entertainment purposes; a good stamping ground. Near the sea were two of our regular haunts, the Beach Club and the Kontiki club, the latter being part of the Sinah Warren, a huge holiday complex with many rich pickings for lusty young men like us.

Jill's parents were fiery and rowed a lot and both were not at home a lot of the time, so we spent some great times at her house, with some fantastic impromptu parties. One night all four of us had had a lot to drink and it seemed a good idea to skinny dip in the sea. It was just too far to walk from Jill's house, so we piled into Jill's yellow Mini and headed for the beach. We all stripped off completely, ran into the sea and frolicked around for a few minutes but the girls soon got cold and we all four ended up naked back in the Mini.

Due to the drink all inhibitions seemed to be shed as Paula and I got naughty in the back while the other two were playing similarly in the front. Space was at a premium, especially as Paula wasn't exactly petite, but although the full Monty didn't happen we had some great rude fun before eventually deciding we would all be more comfortable back at Jill's house. In my experience, girls don't usually do that sort of thing with others around but that night they both did with us all snugly in the mini.

As a matter of fact, Paula and I didn't actually consummate our relationship fully. We did most other things possible but for some reason it never happened. She was just, well, too big for me. She was a lovely girl but didn't turn me on enough. Our relationship fizzled out after a while, though Steve and Jill still saw each other, they seemed to have something going. Well, they did until Steve's real girlfriend, Val, who he thought was safely away working on the other side of the Atlantic in Bermuda, suddenly announced she was returning to the UK. Steve panicked and decided Jill had to go, and quickly. We were due to play football on the Sunday morning and he said he was going to tell her then.

The poor girl, who was very much smitten with Steve, and thought he was with her (well, he was a bit, but...) was alone on the bitterly cold touchline during the game watching him. We went into the changing rooms after the game and I said that surely he wasn't going to tell her then – just like that? He replied he had no choice, Val was on her way, he had to do it. I went out five minutes after him to wait in his car and could see them in a huddle, talking animatedly under a tree.

Eventually he joined me and I could see he was upset, he liked Jill a lot. As we pulled away I caught a glimpse of her sad little face, the tears streaming down her cheeks. Ah, the ways of love!

Forty years on, Steve and I are still good mates and I always remind him of breaking poor Jill's heart. At the time I ribbed him about it for months. As it happened, he didn't last a long time with Val but he never tried to rekindle his relationship with Jill.

He should have.

31. Black Mac... aka Leroy McLaine

Black Mac, as he was known, was of Caribbean origin, shorter than most at about 5ft 4, but solid, dependable and very short-sighted, even seemingly with his glasses. He was very dark-skinned and spoke in a cultured West Indian accent.

He had been the RAF lightweight boxing champion in earlier days but hardly ever talked about it. One night we were watching a fight on the television when Harry Carpenter, the BBC commentator, was on. Someone said something about Carpenter and Mac said quietly to me. 'Huh! Can't stand the bloke, he was damn rude about me!' I asked Mac what he meant .

'Oh, I was boxing in the Inter-Services final and he was commentating for the TV. I was up against a very tall, lanky sailor and I couldn't get near him. He was so much taller and had such long arms. I knew I was losing and as I went back to my corner at the end of the second round, I overheard Carpenter say that it was obvious that I had no class. I wouldn't mind if the bloke was an average height and I could fight him normally but this guy was almost a freak, he was so tall!' Mac slowly shook his head. He didn't say anything else, so of course, I persisted.

'What happened?'

'Oh, I knocked him out in the last round. I was so cross!' he smiled and the sun came out, his teeth were that bright. I liked his modesty. I wouldn't have told the story like that!

One night, in a Portsmouth pub on an early Saturday evening pub crawl, we were all standing at the bar, chatting away, while Mac was intently reading the football 'pink' with all the days results, scanning it intently from only inches away, due to his being as blind as a bat. One of us – not me, as I was a non-smoker – thought it would be a laugh to secretly set light to the bottom of Mac's newspaper. When it was lit, we all nudged each other and slowly backed away while Mac, completely oblivious to everything except the football reports, read on...

The pub was about half-full and quickly everyone, with the exception of Mac, was in on the joke. Even as the flames grew stronger and higher he still didn't notice, until with a scream, he threw the paper down, and jumped all over it, cursing and swearing at us as he put it out. This cabaret act brought the place down, everyone was rolling around laughing, except Mac, although eventually even he saw the funny side of it.

It was Mac who fancied Jean Bull and although he never said anything to me, I got the impression he didn't approve of our relationship, or certainly my part in it, as I was also going out with someone else at the same time. It's a good job it never came to anything, as he would have flattened me, even though I was taller, but Mac and I always seemed to have a good relationship, with mutual respect.

Someone told me that he may have pursued Jean later after she moved to Canada and for all I know they may be together as I write this. That would be nice, as they were two very agreeable, gentle people who I was lucky enough to know for a while in my formative years. God bless them both.

32.   An Hirsute Youth!

Back at school, around 1964, when I was about fifteen, our English master, Stanley Middleton,[7] who I later discovered was a well-known author, came into our classroom and observed one of our number, Pete Jackson, who was illegally sporting longer hair than was allowed whereupon 'Stan' cocked his head to one side and announced, in a reflective way,

'You're looking very hirsute today, Jackson!'

When we asked him what it meant, he told us to look it up. We did and thereafter 'hirsute' became one of our buzzwords, like 'killer', 'zert' and 'mango' (anyone remember what they mean?).

In those days no self-respecting youth I ever went to school with possessed a satchel to carry his books in, we all favoured ex-army haversacks purchased from the Army and Navy stores. These handy carry-alls had a big advantage over any namby-pamby satchel, in that the hinged flap that serves as the protective top of the haversack provided a blank easel on which one's statement to the world could be displayed, usually in Fat Smith's art lesson using the paint provided.

Quite a few lads painted a self-portrait but with desired longer hair adorning the image, thanks to Stan now having imaginative titles like 'Mick the hirsute', or more memorably for me 'An Hirsute Youth' painted underneath. Everybody was 'youth' when I went to school, we all called each other by that name. My individual message creatively said 'MAC', with my painted cartoon of the Golden Wonder crisps mascot, a kilted Scotsman on it but the

---

[7] Stanley Middleton FRSL (1 August 1919 – 25 July 2009) was a British novelist. He was born in Bulwell, Nottinghamshire and educated at High Pavement School, Stanley Road, Nottingham and University College Nottingham. He began writing at university and in 1958 published *A Short Answer*. He taught English at High Pavement Grammar School for many years and was a highly prolific author. In 1974, his novel *Holiday* won the Booker prize. *Her Three Wise Men*, his last and 44th novel, was published in 2008. *Source:* Wikepedia.

word *hirsute* stuck with me. I carried it into the forces with me and still use it today. Stan was a great teacher, incidentally, and a hugely prolific author. I think he won the Booker prize in 1974, ten years after teaching me what 'hirsute' meant.

To put it mildly, hair was huge in the sixties and seventies as a fashion statement and still is today, of course. But pre-services, hardly ever did I dabble in any hirsute experimentation, primarily due to a 'Here's two bob, go and get your hair cut' type of ex-Naval father (I knew where I could get it cut by a Polish barber for one and sixpence and pocket the change). This was coupled with my enthusiastic presence in The Air Training Corps for four years prior to joining the RAF. Consequently long hair hadn't ever grown on my head, nor the idea to grow it inside it, until I was well-established in Her Majesty's superior service.

When it came to hair, our major problem was not really on the camp itself, where I spent four and a half years, but when we stepped outside into civilian life. We were the only RAF station in an area full of Naval establishments, dominated by the home of the Royal Navy, the famous city of Portsmouth, so any civilians out there equated short hair with the Navy and we would do anything rather than admit we were servicemen of any kind – especially not the Navy!

About six months after arrival at my new permanent home on the South Coast, a lad arrived who became a good mate of mine, Tim Simons (you remember, Lorna's husband from Chapter 22 'The Mecca Run'). He was a local lad from Portsmouth's neighbouring town of Gosport. I met his civvy mates, even going on holiday to Cornwall with four of them, and they were a good crowd. Tim himself had a good head of straight black hair, with a sort of natural quiff which made it stick straight out to the front.

Early on in our friendship, as I admired the cut of his hair, he took me down into Portsmouth to his hairdresser friend's salon, where he and his mates had been going for years. This was a new experience for me, not going somewhere alone just to get my hair cut, but in a group atmosphere, passing say a morning or an afternoon, with the latest rude jokes and piss-taking over a period of a few hours while we all had our hair cut.

The owner and our personal hairdresser, Neil, was a bit older and more worldly-wise than we were. His young apprentices, who cut hair under his expert tuition, were usually the butt of his very sarcastic humour but he could also turn his sights on us if the situation arose.

One leave I had spent a couple of weeks away at home in Nottingham and had gone on a blind date with a friend of my mate Andy's girlfriend. She turned out to be a randy little hairdresser called Dee who offered, amongst other services, to cut my hair. I let her and it got very sexual afterwards. My new haircut seemed fine to me but later back at camp, with Dee and my short-but-passionate tryst subsided, for the moment at least, it was back to Neil I went with the lads several weeks later.

Neil's chair was in the middle of the salon, like a king in his court, surrounded by his courtiers. Down two sides were the apprentices' cutting chairs and seats provided for the customers on the other two sides, so Neil's chair was a kind of central throne affair. When it was my turn, Neil said not a word as I climbed into the chair. He wrapped the white cloth round me, tucking it in firmly so only my head poked out. He then proceeded to pump the chair pedal with his foot, so that I rose higher and higher, far more than was necessary, until I seemed a head and shoulders above everyone. Then he stepped back to be with the other lads I had come with, folding his arms gravely.

His language was always very colourful, usually even worse than ours, and that was saying something. At last he spoke.

'Fuggin' 'ell, Mac!' he exclaimed emphatically and loudly as he gazed at me in awe, slowly shaking his head in disbelief. 'Who the fug's cut your hair?'

In those days I blushed easily and could feel myself going purple, unable to do anything but squirm, high up on my pedestal, as the whole place sniggered, awaiting my answer.

'Erm... well Neil... actually... it was this bird I've been going out with...' I tried to make this sound reasonable but any answer was dangerous with Neil, who could slay you with his tongue.

'Well I just hope for your sake she fugs better than she cuts hair!'

That brought the place down, completing my humiliation.

Neil's expert grooming meant that we always looked smart and tidy, if a fair bit longer than regulation, but we could get away with it where we worked.

By the way, just for the record, the answer to his observation? Well, yes, I think she probably did; no complaints there...

I played in various football teams in my time in the RAF, usually in the station second team, as I wasn't quite good enough to play regularly for the first, where we had such good players as striker Kenny Oram and goalkeeper 'Garth' Hawkins, who both played for the RAF. We usually only played Navy teams in our league, but one cruel winter's day in the cup we played an Art College from somewhere in West Sussex. The whole match was a complete farce for two reasons. The first was the awful weather, strong winds and blinding rain turning the pitch into a quagmire, but the biggest laugh was hair, or more precisely, the contrast of it. Being an Art College, hardly any of the opposition had hair that wasn't shoulder length, some had headbands, plaits and pony-tails, and a few actually appeared to be able to see the ball during the game. In direct and seemingly ridiculous contrast, we resembled 'a bunch of escaped convicts' as one of our lads described us.

During this ridiculous game, we were better than them in almost every way, but we just couldn't score. Their goalie performed miracles under the conditions to keep us out. Five minutes from a goalless end, we got a penalty. My mate Steve, who was technically banned at the time but illegally playing under an assumed name, as we were short at the time – but we won't go into that – stepped up to take it. Their soaked, saturated mud-covered goalie peered through his hair and the pouring rain as Steve roared up to the ball, only to smash it straight at him but the ball was rising all the time and went straight between the goalie's upstretched arms, just over his head and under the bar, so we won 1-0. When it was pointed out afterwards in the changing rooms that it was the worst taken penalty we had ever seen, Steve shrugged and said 'I was just trying to part his hair for him!'

When at last my five years in the RAF were drawing to a close, I wangled a resettlement course which, coupled with my terminal leave, meant I was able to leave the RAF over two months before my actual release date. I still had to officially 'clear', which meant one full day back after all my final leave was over, for handing my kit in and administratively leaving the Air Force for good, although I was still on the reserve for three more years, unpaid, of course...

During this lengthy period of resettlement and terminal leave in early 1972, I at last grew my hair longer, for the first time ever and also – a beard! As my hair is naturally black and curly I looked like a Rastafarian after a while but as time for me to return to the RAF for my last final day to clear approached, I went to a real men's hairdresser's where they shaped and cut my hair and beard in a modern trendy style. I thought I looked terrific as I returned to camp and all the lads admired the new Mac, the one ready for civilian life.

However, I had forgotten one vital fact. I was still not out of the services until the next day. A *clearance chit* was required, which had to be dutifully filled in with a great many signatures before I could finally take my leave of the RAF – and the very first signature on the list was that of the most feared man on camp, the Station Warrant Officer (SWO), of whom I have spoken before, he of the shaved head and immaculate appearance, who was the scourge of us scruffies *up the line* and could engender fear in us from afar.

The big question now was – should I go and see him first and brave the lion in his den? The answer, which may have cost me dearly, was no I didn't. I decided to mop up a few easy ones like the cold weather store to take my airfield protective stuff back and suchlike, but I didn't get very far without trouble. I strolled nonchalantly into Bedding Control to take my sheets, blankets and pillows back when I walked slap-bang into a real shiny sergeant, a very nasty piece of work.

'Who the fuggin' ell do you think you are, then?' he snarled.

'I'm SAC McGregor, sergeant, I've just come to cl...'

He cut me for dead.

'Not with hair like that and a fuggin' beard you're not! Get down the barber's and get that lot off!'

'But sergeant,' I persisted, 'I've only come to clear...'

I just managed to get this in before he erupted.

'Did you hear what I said?' he screamed. 'You've got one hour – if you're not back by then with that lot off, you're on a charge'.

He abruptly turned on his heel and strode away.

I was distraught, almost in tears at the unfairness of it all. I had only one card left to play and made straight for the SWO's office. The purpose was to throw myself on his mercy and appeal against this grave injustice. There was a slight chance, not good, admittedly but worth taking. I knocked on his office door and a voice that came from about fifteen feet underground told me to enter. Without his trademark hat he looked even more terrifying – not one of the silver grey hairs on his head could have been longer than a quarter of an inch. He stared at me unnervingly and asked me why I was there. I told him the story of my one last day and related the sad story of the unreasonable over-zealous sergeant forcing me to get my haircut on my last day.

I finished blathering and waited. After considering my plight he smiled and asked for my clearance chit, which had about five signatures on it. He looked at it and shook his head sadly. I knew then I was doomed. He gazed at me, almost pityingly.

'Whose name is at the top of this list, son ?' he asked quietly.

'Yours, sir.'

'Then why haven't you come to me first then, son?'

As he spoke, I could see which way this was going. Before I had a chance to reply, he went on. 'If you had come to see me first and I'd cleared you, I might have been able to do something but as you haven't and you've now received a direct order from an NCO, I think you'd better carry it out – don't you, son ?'

Helpless and out of aces, I knew he was right. The system, the Forces, the RAF, Catch 22 had all got the better of me – and on my last day!

In four and a half years I had skilfully avoided paying a visit to *the camp barber* (a brutal sheep-shearer in a white coat who only knew one way to cut your hair – to sharpen your head to be more precise). I wasn't about to let him loose on my new crowning glory. I jumped into my car, sped off and found a human being in a men's hairdressers on the other side of town.

'What can I do for you then, my friend?' he asked.

'Please tidy this up with the very minimum forces-style cut possible, and ... shave my beard off please.'

I was near to tears.

'Oh dear,' he said sympathetically. 'Like that is it?'

'Worse – don't ask.' But I told him the whole saga anyway, while he cut my hair and shaved off my beard and inside twenty painful minutes, once more I was visually back in the Royal Air Force. My hour was almost up as I walked back into Bedding Control. Before I could say anything, a triumphant grin greeted me.

'That's better!' My tormenter almost laughed, the sick bastard. 'Now you actually look like a serviceman. What was it you wanted, anyway?'

The worst bit was that sooner or later I had to run the gauntlet of my mates, most of course having seen and admired the new Mac – civilian style. Some duly fell about and extracted the urine at my humiliation. Mickey-taking was always part of service-life. It was expected and you got little in the way of sympathy.

A couple of close mates were genuinely sorry for me, saying that you could never beat the system, which to a certain extent is true. As it happened, I went from the RAF fairly quickly into the selling profession, where long hair and scruffiness were not acceptable either, so soon it was back to square one with my hair again and apart from one or two skirmishes later on I never re-grew the beard either – such is life!

Long hair you say? Well, here's the truth,
I never was an hirsute youth!

33. Shiny Stories – Remembrance Day

'Hey, Mac! That's Aylott broken down, isn't it? I levered myself up gingerly from my seat on the coach and looked out of the nearside window, as we passed a Mini stopped at the side of the road. The bonnet was up with my 'mate' Paul Aylott forlornly gazing into the engine, hands on hips. Why was that, then?

Every year in November, the nearest Sunday to the 11th was Remembrance Day and we provided a unit of the RAF to march to The Cenotaph in Portsmouth with our Navy and Army colleagues to honour our war dead. In November down on the South Coast it always seemed to be freezing with a bitterly cold wind blowing and we were grateful for our big greatcoats. Once I was actually on the parade, I never minded it. Our SWO used to crank us up just before we set off, with muttered comments like 'bags of swank lads' and 'come on boys, you're representing the Royal Air Force now. Shoulders up, chests out, swing those arms!' which we did, proudly rising to the occasion to represent our senior branch of Her Majesty's forces, to compete with those second division ones.

During my time in the RAF I did it every year but, in fact, I shouldn't have. The system worked like this. Every station had certain numbers of airmen in each trade and rank and depending how many of you were the same – say four of you – theoretically you would only do one Remembrance Day every four years. Don't ask me what happened if you were the only trade of your kind, I don't know if you did every one. 'Tough shit' would be the standard retort from everyone if you did. In my case the bloke I was posted to Thorney island with was Paul Aylott, who I shared the *Prospect of Whitby* experience with, and more. He and I were the only two of the same rank and trade on the station, so by rights we should have shared such duties – but we didn't!

To my steadily increasing annoyance, he slid out of every one, with various excuses that ensured I had to do the parades – and every year my resentment festered and grew. By 1971 I had only four months to go and was certain that this year I would not be doing it. But yet again he pulled it off. I can't remember why but my name was down for it once again. Just to make matters doubly worse, I knew he had a much-coveted weekend job in a petrol station, so it really got me that he would be earning extra money while I was freezing my Max Walls off on a parade that he should have been doing instead of me! But what could I do?

Well... it was like this, your honour. I have already documented elsewhere what we did on a Saturday night when we were on parade or had duties on a Sunday. The early evening bus down into the town was taken, we either went on a pub crawl ending up in The Railway Tavern, or you just stayed in The Railway all evening, ending up pissed and catching the last bus back; not a lot of difference really. So, that night before my last-ever Remembrance Day parade, I was downtown getting well and truly rat-arsed, getting in a steadily grimmer mood with Aylott as the evening progressed.

By the time I was safely on the last bus, my mood was funereal. How had I let this happen – again? I got off the bus and wove my unsteady path over the dark, quiet car park that led to the blocks where we all lived. At this point I would point out that I have what my capacious father referred to as 'a Woolworths' bladder', meaning that I could not hold anything bladder-wise like the amount of alcoholic liquor he could – in fact nobody could, he was well-known for it. Sadly, I did not inherit his incredible capacity and was bursting to go for a wee. It was then I spotted Aylott's yellow Mini over in a very dark corner of the car park...

Next morning I was nursing a king-sized hangover and had to be woken several times by the other lads on parade. At that time I had a fearsome reputation for being extremely terse and monosyllabic when spoken to first thing in the morning. Most people understood and respected that. I usually came round about mid-morning and became a human being again but this morning I was in a black rage at having to get up, wash, shave and make myself look like an upright member of Her Majesty's Services when I felt so bad. I could remember little of what had happened the previous night past about nine o'clock and didn't want to anyway, just having to get up was bad enough. Knowing my body and its needs,

I dragged myself to the mess for a standard RAF greasy breakfast, washed down with cups of tea, until I felt marginally better.

After putting on our Best Blue uniforms and greatcoats we trundled over to the waiting coach where our presence was officially noted by the usually fearsome SWO as he took our names and ticked them off on his list. I slumped into a seat near the back on my own, hoping to doze for the thirty-minute journey into Portsmouth. The coach slowly lumbered out onto the main road to take us off the camp and we had only gone five hundred yards and were passing the married quarters when my attention was alerted. I looked out of the window and saw Aylott standing at the side of his car, like a giant pissed-off Teddy Bear (he was a fat bastard), wondering why his pride and joy wouldn't go...

The next day I was having my lunch in the mess when Aylott came up with a foul expression on his face.

'Do you know, somebody pissed in my petrol tank?'

My time had come...

'No, but you hum it and I'll play it!'

Guffaws all round from my mates.

Aylott grimaced but went on. 'I don't suppose you'd know anything about it?'

I tried not to laugh.

'Me? Why should I know anything about it?'

And that was that. He couldn't prove anything. It could have been anyone. It had happened before, we all knew the story – the time when an RAF policeman, who was heartily disliked by everyone for booking them for anything, made the huge mistake of leaving the soft top off his MG Midget one warm evening when the lads returned from the pub, steaming drunk...

But mine was the kingdom, the power and the glory when I was given the chance, once again, to proudly represent the Royal Air Force in Portsmouth, home of the Royal Navy on Remembrance Sunday. Chest filled with pride, I did my bit. *Per Ardua ad Astra!*

34.   The Worst Day of My Life

'Oh, I can't do that one, I'm playing in a cup match tomorrow evening,' said brainbox Steve, he of the 'Let's get a little job when we're on leave and earn us some extra cash – beats lying in your pit for two weeks.' That last bit was aimed at me, as I would take most opportunities to doss around at that age (about twenty). As it happened, we were already on our second job with the casual work agency we had contacted. Steve had put paid to our first job as temporary labour when, bored, he had borrowed a spanner to fix a pallet truck and nearly brought the place to a standstill.

The actual maintenance man, whose job it was to do such repairs, went ballistic when he found out, complaining bitterly about some casual labourer (the lowest of the low) taking away his livelihood, so we were unceremoniously chucked out of what *had* been shaping up to be a doddle. Having been hired to help move heavy plant around it transpired that the company that had taken us on was not quite ready and was therefore paying us to sit around waiting – until Handy Harry stuck his oar in.

Back at the agency, we were offered two separate driving jobs, one of which might involve a little extra overtime in the early evening. Of course, Pele was not available, due to his footballing career, so this job fell to me. Little did I know what I was in letting myself in for. The next morning I reported to a decorating wholesalers warehouse near Portsmouth. They showed me what looked a rather large truck to me and showed me the controls. No real problems but as I had never driven anything larger than a Vauxhall Victor before, I was a little apprehensive, although I tried not to show it (service to Queen and Country and all that).

With the benefit of hindsight, I can see now how I was set up. For my first trip they bunged a few rolls of paper and several tins of paint in the back and told me to take them to an adjacent new housing estate under construction. I easily found my target, unloaded and was back in the depot in forty-five minutes. They sent me happily to the canteen, where I was fed a delicious bacon roll and mug of tea. The old dear in charge of the canteen shook her head. 'It's hard, that job you're doing, isn't it? The last lad from the Navy only lasted a week.'

'Well, if you will employ second-class servicemen!' I said. I loved that one.

Every couple of minutes someone would pop their head round the door and say something like: 'Do you know Portchester/ Fareham / Titchfield / wherever?' and I would say 'No, but I'll find it' and everyone seemed happy. Eventually I was told all was ready. I was given various maps of the area and a clipboard with many delivery sheets attached to it, about thirty-odd, I think. As I swung myself up into the cab, someone shouted,

'You might have to go to the other depot at Christchurch later. We'll leave a message for you at your last drop. Do you know Christchurch?'

'I'll find it,' I answered cockily, as I drove my way out of the yard and lumbered out in the suggested direction of my first drop. My wagon was completely full, not a square inch to spare. The calls were almost all small DIY stores or the odd ironmongery store. I had only completed two reasonably successful drops before I hit my first big spot of trouble.

Just outside town I took a wrong turning and realised I needed to be going back in the opposite direction. I swung into a narrow lane to find myself about to go under a low hump-backed railway bridge. Too low and I hit it! Fortunately, due to my unfamiliar surroundings and temporary loss of direction, I was not going fast, but the impact and noise rocked me as I stopped immediately. For a horrible minute I thought I had wedged the truck under the bridge but with some violent reversing I shot back and, apart from dents at the top of the wagon and a few bruised bricks on the bridge, I got away with it. Doing a ninety-nine point turn in the narrow lane was very difficult but I eventually got back on my way.

My next problem was caused by failing to secure the cages after I had loosened them to facilitate a particular delivery. When I next opened the sliding vertical metal door, several litres of sticky brilliant white gloss had been catapulted across the floor, making it very difficult to get in and out without attracting white markings on my shoes and clothes. I left one manager incandescent with rage as he was urgently awaiting his delivery. Before I could stop him, he jumped in to get his order and ended up with white sticky, glossy streaks over his dark trousers and black shiny shoes.

It got steadily worse. I then forgot to put the heavy electrically operated metal tail ramp back up. As I drove across Southampton I vaguely heard loud crashes coming from the rear and wondered what they were until it dawned on me what I had done.

The rest of the morning was a blur; the long, hard schedule left no time for pleasantries like lunch or a drink. I was glad I'd had the tea and bacon roll at nine am. I vaguely wondered how Steve was getting on. What was it he was delivering? Cooking oil wasn't it? Sounded messy.

All afternoon I soldiered (airmaned?) on, the load gradually lessening. About five-thirty, now right over on the farthest side of Southampton from home, I reached my last drop where, sure enough, I was told, 'There's a message from your office. Can you go to the Christchurch depot, pick up some empty pallets and bring them back?'

'Where is Christchurch?' I asked, and was sent out on the Bournemouth road, going still further away from home. Have you ever been to Christchurch? Another half-hour took me into this very twee, picturesque Hampshire town, with its pretty, narrow little streets – just what I didn't need. I was lost, when a car coming in the opposite direction flashed his lights and the driver shouted, 'If you're looking for your depot, you're going the wrong way. Turn round, back to the lights, right and second left'.

'Oh great, thank you – turn around? Oh yeah, how?'

I was getting tired and irritable now. I roared off down the road and spotted a small public car park on my right. I swung in. The car park was long and narrow with the same entrance and exit. Some cars were parked in two rows down the middle. I needed to swing right round and as I moved down the left side I saw a reasonable looking gap in the middle of the cars, big enough for me to make a complete U-turn and head back to the exit where I had come in.

I dragged the big steering wheel round to make a complete right hand lock but as I turned sharply I heard a loud bang and, looking back out of my driver's side window, I saw a Morris Marina bouncing across the car park with a bent wing. Normally I would have stopped but I pretended I had not noticed it. As there didn't seem to be anyone about, I sped off to find the depot, which I found fairly easily, the directions were good. The pallets were loaded rapidly and I hurtled back onto the Southampton road. By now it was seven in the evening and I had had enough.

Unfortunately more drama occurred when I realised I was almost out of fuel. I had used the whole tankful I had started out with. I vaguely remembered being told that I would be reimbursed if necessary, so I paid for £5 worth of petrol to get me back to the depot. It was gone eight-thirty by the time I reached the depot. There was no-one about as I let myself in, unlocking the padlock with a key I found on the truck's key ring and parked the wagon in the yard.

I had a last look at the truck. In the excitement back in Christchurch I had forgotten to examine the side of the chassis where now I saw that there was a considerable dent and a scrape. Coupled with the damage to the top I had done earlier, the truck looked as though it had come through a war zone and I felt as if I had too! After locking up, I put the keys through the letterbox and let myself out in my car before snapping the padlock.

Heading back to camp I experienced a range of feelings, starving hunger, tiredness bordering on exhaustion, rage, humiliation and homicidal thoughts. The object of the last thoughts was lying on his pit, watching football on TV when I got back.

'Hi Mac,' He didn't even drag his eyes away from the action. 'You're late. Did you go down the pub? What a doddle my job is. I've been delivering cooking oil to cafés and fish and chip shops. Most of the customers gave me a cup of tea or a bacon roll. I must have had a dozen! I was getting through the calls too quickly, so they told me to slow down. 'Go and sit on the beach for an hour, Steve,' they said, so I did. You should have been there Mac, the girls were amazing, there was this blonde one with big boobs who smiled and said...'

I won't go on, it hurts too much. Of course, I didn't get paid for that awful day and to add insult to injury it cost me the petrol money. Luckily they didn't come after me for the damage I did to the truck, although via the agency they threatened to. I still feel guilty about the Morris Marina. I know those cars were ugly and awful but he didn't deserve that, did he?

As for Steve and me, amazingly I spared his life and we are still good mates, some forty years on but I never, ever let him forget that day. And it was all so unnecessary – if only he hadn't borrowed that spanner, he could have saved me from one of the worst days of my life!

35. Hi de Hi!

Smoothie Mac was waxing lyrical on our favourite subject – women and how to get them.

'You can't go wrong – even you lot!' he said, disparagingly.

Mac was our guru, the epitome of how to do it – the trouble was, he held all the cards that most of us didn't. For a start he was at least five to seven years older than us. I think he was twenty five, tall, dark and exceedingly handsome – with a sports car and a very confident way with women which seemed to sweep them off their feet. He had it all – and used it to devastating effect.

Where we 'couldn't go wrong' was the latest place he and his hunting partner, the giant Bradley, had found to pick up women easily – Butlin's! The well-known holiday camp was in Bognor, about sixteen miles away and was somewhere we had never considered. So it was that on the next possible night out, at about nine o'clock, with a few pints inside us for Dutch courage, my mate Steve and I found ourselves skulking around the Butlin's perimeter fence in a Bognor back street. We followed Mac's instructions to the letter, which ran along the following lines:

'It's like a reverse Colditz – you walk along 'til you find a quiet bit on both sides of the fence, there's usually hedges and trees about. One of you pulls up the wire enough for the other to roll under, then he does the same until you're both in. Just straighten up, brush yourself down, then casually join the other holiday-makers and get on with it – there's bars, shows, discos – you can't go wrong! Well, we didn't go wrong, it was as easy as that, and we did it a number of times with varying success.

In my case it was early on in my affairs with women, I was not long out of training and I had a lot to learn. In, I think, my second attempt I picked up a pretty young girl called Christine, on holiday with her family, who were from Stevenage. It was right at the end of her holiday but we kept in touch by phone and letter and after a few weeks I went up in my little car *The Pig* to spend the weekend with her. She told me she was seventeen, going on eighteen and doing her 'A' levels at school, and loved it when I was waiting outside her school to pick her up on the Friday afternoon.

We hadn't slept together but it was nearing and I proposed she then came up to my home town of Nottingham for the weekend, where I was sure I could swing it one way or another. However, at the start of the week prior to the proposed weekend she became elusive on the phone, her parents telling me she was 'out' when I rang. After two days I finally managed to speak to her, when she cried and said it was 'all in the letter'. Obviously it was a 'Dear John'. Enough said, but by now I realised all was not well and managed to drag the truth out of her – that she was really fourteen, not seventeen. She wanted to sleep with me but her parents could see problems with her education and advised her strongly to end it with me. I was astounded. I had no doubt at all that she was seventeen, she certainly looked and acted like it to me.

I duly received the letter, which asked me to wait until she was sixteen, keeping in touch, but there was no way I was going to go out with a fourteen-year-old. I wrote back and told her, in mock outrage, that I had been deceived and that was that. I then received a letter from her elder sister, begging me to keep in touch as Christine was very upset and off school, but I decided not to respond and just get on with my life. Plenty more fish in the sea, as they say, especially on the South Coast.

Isn't it funny/sad/happy (delete where applicable when you hear certain records and they bring back strange special memories you had forgotten. Christine and I loved *Massachusetts* by the Bee Gees; I bought it for her and we played it incessantly. Whenever I hear it played, I think of her. I wonder if it reminds her of me?

Soon afterwards things got a lot better at Butlin's for me, with a randy young red-haired lady from Scotland called Sandra, who knew what chalets were for after dark. Not having been intimate – or even out with – a redhead before, I needed to know what all young men wonder – does the colour extend – well, everywhere – if you catch my drift? To help me in my quest for carnal knowledge Sandra wore the shortest tartan mini-skirt I have ever seen. Even if she gently coughed you could see her knickers, which were white, not tartan but definitely not virginal. With her strong Scottish accent it was difficult to understand her at times, but in the disco when the slowies came on all talking ceased, and we soon disappeared back to her place for an interesting and satisfying hour or two. As it was dark initially and other matters were (much) more urgent I had to wait a little while before I found the answer I needed to know, which was – yes! Fascinatingly red – well, ginger – it was too! It made up for the disappointment with Christine and meant that every time I watched *Hi-de-Hi* I was able to reply Ho de Ho! with feeling and remember the tartan miniskirt and the red and white underneath it. Hoots mon!

36. Prospect of Witlessness

In the RAF, when you are 'posted' (transferred to another station) there are strange dark forces at work. Just where, why, when and, most baffling, by whom such things are decided is a question to which few know the answer and even if they do, they keep it very quiet. It is almost perverse how some go here and others go there, contrary to their wishes, it seems in many cases. In my short RAF career it only happened to me once but, like most young men who experienced it, the move changed my life.

From the fourteen-odd who passed our course, only a quarter, including me, went to a camp considered a plum posting. Most of the half-dozen Londoners on our course were mortified when, having applied for southern postings, they were sent to 'V' bomber stations in flat, windswept Lincolnshire or worse, the extreme north of Scotland, whereas I, a Midlands boy from Nottingham was sent south to an idyllic station like Thorney Island, considered a 'plum posting'. Mind you, in true forces fashion I certainly rubbed cockney noses in it, as you learn to do quickly – anyone remember Harry Belafonte's 'Island in the Sun'? My calypso version went:

> Thorney Island in the sun,
> Willed to me by the postings man.

Usually accompanied by cockney shouts of 'Fugg off, you jammy Nottingham prat!' Hee hee, what fun!

There was one downside, however, in that I was accompanied by one other member of my course, a Londoner, as it happened. Had I any say in the matter, which of course I didn't, he would have been in the top three I would not have chosen. During the time of my trade training, for personal reasons I have listed elsewhere, I was extremely uptight in temperament. This guy, Paul Aylott, was one of life's practical jokers, a big clumsy bear of a bloke whose favourite trick, if you unluckily happened to be near him in a swimming pool, would be try to drown you by heaving himself on you and forcing you down – he tried with me several times. I couldn't abide his jokey, cockney, matey manner. I think it showed during the course and normally we kept our distance.

But fate took a hand and we were sent together to this envied posting, on an island off the South Coast, in 1967. As I hadn't passed my test yet, before we were due to report to our new station one weekend we took my car, the wonderful Pig back to my parent's house in Nottingham, hitched back to camp and travelled down to our new home in his big old Austin A55. Paul and I were sent to work together in the radio servicing bay, on permanent days from eight until five every day. It seemed we got on a little better away from the pressures of training, so much so that one weekend he invited me to stay with his family, meet his mates and see a bit of London.

I went for the last bit really; London has always fascinated me, still does, and we went to stay the weekend at his mother's tiny terraced house in Ilford. I don't really recall too much about his Mum, but on the Saturday morning we travelled down to meet his mates in central London, which was quite an experience.

The first surprise was that two of Paul's mates' fathers were Beefeaters, who lived and worked in the Tower of London. Their grace-and-favour houses were actually part of The Tower, so the families must have lived, ate and breathed their occupations. I seem to remember they even had their own pub. We went round to see one friend, who had a garage literally 'underneath the arches'. I had seen such places on television but never in person, so it was an experience. But the real surprise, nay culture shock, was that Paul and his mates were all rockers, real motorbike greasers, who lived for their bikes and leathers.

I vaguely remembered Paul mentioning it previously but I had no idea of the scale of their devotion. Massive Triumph Bonnevilles were the order of the day and Solvol Autosol was used in quantity to shine the chrome on their machines. I did not dare breathe that in an earlier life I had been a scooter-riding Mod back in my home town of Nottingham, with a Lambretta first and later a Vespa, festooned with umpteen mirrors. I had short, clean hair and wore a Parka, Italian suits, desert boots and Ben Sherman shirts. Fortunately they seemed ok with me, accepting that I was just an

RAF mate of their friend. We related funny service-based stories to them and all laughed together.

It was suggested that we go out for a pub-crawl on the Saturday evening to the East End, which sounded good to me. The four of us included two equally brawny mates of Paul's and after a couple of pubs someone suggested we went to the *Prospect of Whitby* pub. I had never heard of it but I was told that this was a place where you had fun and there was an amazing atmosphere. The radical trendy Tariq Ali often held court there, so off we went. This famous old waterside pub was at the bottom of a blind cul-de-sac, right on the river Thames, in the old docklands. It certainly was a lively place, with music, laughter and some lovely, pretty girls.

As we had had a few drinks, a silly game developed where we all stood at the bottom of a big staircase, with huge stone pillars either side. When a nice-looking girl, or better still a group of them, came down, someone would stick out their foot and trip them and the others would catch them, enjoying a little close female physical contact. Simple, harmless and just a bit of fun – but then disaster struck!

I was 'tripping' and before I realised what I was doing, a bloke went over my foot. He was smaller than me but a few years older (I was eighteen and would put him somewhere around the mid-twenties). He didn't like it, or me, and thrust his face belligerently in mine and demanded to know why I had tried to trip him up. I was in no mood for his aggression and took a sarcastic attitude.

'Listen,' I said menacingly. 'Why would *I* try to trip *you* up?'

He told me not to try to get funny with him and repeated his question, but louder. I really blew it then when I told him firmly to fuck off, adding 'sonny' at the end, just to put a bit of spice in it.

His face contorted with rage.

'You will regret that,' he spat, before disappearing. I laughed it off with the others, who had hardly noticed, but a few minutes later something hit me hard on my shoulder, spinning me round. I was confronted by the biggest, fattest, ugliest, spottiest yob I had ever seen. He grabbed me tightly by my lapels and pulled me closer to his vile pizza face and spelt out slowly but very menacingly.

'I don't want to talk to you or discuss anything with you. I just want you to come outside – NOW!'

My (good!) mate Paul tried to intervene, innocently asking.

'What's the problem, mate? We only came in here for a quiet drink.' Whereupon Quasimodo dropped me, turned and, seizing Paul's collar and tie in one giant fist, shook him as if he were a toy. With considerable alarm, I heard Paul's head hit the stone pillar behind him. On either side of Quaz were about six equally-large, equally-ugly specimens, leering at us and making threatening gestures. Two huge bouncers suddenly appeared, making the most unhelpful suggestion I have ever heard.

'Come on lads, if you want to fight, go outside.'

I felt faint as I realised there was only one way out, the way we had come in. Quaz hissed to me that they would be waiting for us outside and the lynch-mob dispersed, thank God. But it was getting dangerously near to closing time and every time we peeked out of the one and only door, it seemed more undesirables had been added to the leering crowd waiting for us. I fast-forwarded to waking up the next morning in the Thames.

The same two bouncers approached, this time telling everyone to go home, as the pub was closing shortly. Fast running out of options, we threw ourselves on their mercy and pleaded for help. They asked us where our car was (50 yards up the lane) and, bless 'em, they said they would walk with us. No guarantees but they didn't think the gang would attack us if they were there. The six of us walked out (four trembling between two), our would-be attackers flexing their muscles and leering at us on either side. For a horrible moment, I thought the crowd was going to rush us – but they didn't. We moved slowly up the lane and, surprise-surprise, about thirty yards behind us came the lynch mob.

'Which is your car?' muttered the lead bouncer.

'The green A55 up the road on the left,' said Paul.

'When I say NOW!' our protector whispered. 'Run like hell, get in and drive off, and NEVER, EVER come back here again! We'll try and dissuade 'em but there's a lot of them, so we probably won't be able to stop 'em all.'

At the command we went like hell and thank God Paul's car, unlike my own, was well maintained and started first time. A few stones came our way as we roared away, but luckily there was no further damage. To prove what good lads they were, Paul's mates didn't hold it against me and we spent some more time with them on the Sunday before returning to camp in the evening.

I did once return to The Prospect of Whitby, about fifteen years later, one lunchtime. In daylight things looked very different, much less threatening than I remembered. It was a lovely pub and restaurant in a smashing spot. But that night I could well have been fished out of the river the next day. I was a bit more careful and less 'witless' after that, especially being lippy and calling older lads than me 'sonny!' It improved my Prospects no end!

37. Exodus

The phone rang in the crew room and someone nonchalantly answered with, 'Yeah, ok... I'll tell him,' before ringing off. He turned and saw me. 'Oh, there you are Mac. You've got to report to P3 in SHQ...'

My blood ran cold. Summonses to the dreaded SHQ, – citadel of all things and people shiny and dangerous – were not at all welcome to scruffy, hirsute erks like me at the best of times but this time a terrible foreboding swiftly spread over me. Had I been found out? Was my huge bluff about to be called? Could I talk my way out of it? Why had I done such a stupid thing? How long in the glasshouse was I looking at? Could I plead drunkenness? Insanity?

About a year before I was due to leave the service of Her Majesty, a new regulation was brought in called *Resettlement Leave*, introduced to aid servicemen leaving the forces to obtain a civilian job. How it worked was like this. You found a civilian company or business that was prepared to train you into a new position and you were allowed to have up to four weeks paid leave, up to three months prior to your release date. The idea was that the forces were paying you, so the company didn't need to. Provided the place of work was not within ten miles of a Navy, Army or Air Force establishment, where you could stay every night, you were also paid 'Rate One' payments for overnight accommodation.

This presented an opportunity to leave the services a month earlier than normal with a considerable pay-off, really a wonderful chance to put one over on the system and too good to be missed. The trouble was – what to do? Where to start? I only knew one brave lad who did pull it off but in reality most just let it go – but me? Oh, it nagged at me. I hate missing great opportunities, so – what to do?

Before I explain what happened, I need to clarify something else. My elder sister and her husband had often invited me to stay with them in their new house in a Midlands village, having moved up from Swansea (resting-place of The Pig). As I hadn't taken them up on it before, nearing resettlement time I phoned and asked if I could stay 'for a couple of weeks'. My sister, bless her, said yes straight away, anytime, whatever, she made it all very easy for me. So this venue, well away from service establishments, was ideal. Now all I needed was a four-week job.

About eight weeks before my final date for release, I got a copy of the application form for resettlement leave. It looked remarkably straightforward, relatively brief, an arse-covering piece of paper which basically asked for your number, rank and name, how long and what dates you intended your 'course' to run for, who the company was offering the course, where and what type of work it was and – very importantly, I thought – would the company allow a visit from the RAF to check progress? The only other thing required was a signature from the company and the position of the signatory.

I dwelt long and hard over this short form. A couple of weeks before my applied-for start date and keeping it very quiet, with only a couple of true confidantes knowing, after a few drinks one night I filled it in. As he had a different surname, I stated that my brother-in-law was the proprietor of a garage in the village he lived in and that he was giving me a four-week course in motor mechanics – which was a laugh as I was and am still to this day, useless with cars and their engines. After a few more drinks, filled with bravado and alcohol, I ticked the box saying no visits allowed, forged my brother-in-law's signature and, very late and very drunkenly, put the form into the station's internal mailbox.

The next day it was too late to retrieve it, so I just put it out of my mind, tried to forget it and not worry. Which I did – until the phone rang and I got the summons to SHQ.

I shot back to the block where I lived and tried, as we all did in those dangerous circumstances, to tart myself up and try, at least temporarily, to look like a reasonable member of the Royal Air Force. It wasn't a 'Clarke Kent' moment, going into a phone box looking a normal-looking nerd and coming out transformed into Superman but with a quick wash and shave, clean shirt, tie (a rarity) and a beret to hide some of my black curly hair, it was a reasonable attempt to look semi-normal. There was a 'back way' into SHQ, avoiding some of the knee-length revealing bushes adorning immaculately swept pathways where one felt so vulnerable, and I successfully negotiated my back-door entry into the immaculate corridors of power without any trouble. I arrived nervously at the chest-high counter of the main administration office. The nearest clerk, who I sometimes played football with, looked up and smiled.

'Hi Mac, got some papers for you to sign.' He reached into his tray and went through some other bundles until he found mine. 'Sign here, here, here, here and here.' Anyone in the forces is used to this. We always joked that we signed our lives away in the RAF and after he stamped them in various places, he gave me several back, clipped together.

'Ok, Mac. Take these to the cash office and good luck on your course'. I nodded dumbly and took the papers down another passage to a glass hatch in the wall with a sign over it saying 'Cash Office'. It was closed. With shaking hand, I knocked on the glass. After what seemed a lifetime, the window shot open and a bespectacled spotty face peered out. God, he was ugly. Should he be allowed out in public with spots like that?

'Yes?'

'Erm, I've got these,' I showed him my newly-acquired papers.

' Oh... right.' He snatched them from me.

I tried very hard not to look panic-stricken as he reached for his little machine and stared to add up figures. After what seemed like a lifetime as he double-checked his calculations he suddenly produced from somewhere a small receipt book, wrote something in it and told me to sign the page. As I did so, he opened a drawer, pulled out a bundle of £5 notes and counted them out, finally a couple of £1 notes and some coins as well.

You know that rare moment when the one-arm bandit suddenly pays out? All the bells line up and the machine starts coughing up money. I felt sure someone was behind me, watching me, about to pounce. From memory, it was about £350, more, much more, than I had ever held in my hand before. The most expensive car I had ever bought in those days cost £80. The payment was made up of two months' pay, which was four weeks terminal leave and four weeks resettlement leave, plus a month's *rate ones* for accommodation and some other travelling expenses the RAF had thoughtfully allowed for.

The upshot was that from the day I started my 'training course', in one week's time, I had only one more day's service left, when I had to return, hand in all my uniform, etc and 'clear' the RAF for good. I signed everything and was given one copy of my original document that started it all. I stuffed the money in my pocket and beat a hasty retreat, without looking back, almost as if running from the scene of the crime. I only had a week or so to arrange my departure and have a quick couple of piss-ups with the lads. I said my temporary goodbyes and then loaded all my worldly goods into my lovely little Standard Ten and headed north to the Midlands, feeling as if I'd won the pools.

I quickly adapted to civilian life with my sister and her husband. It was 1972 and they had some great young neighbours and friends, – one friendly wife along the road called Sue I got on *particularly* well with. At a party at their house late one Saturday evening we were dancing snugly in the subdued light of the lounge when she took my hand and before I knew where we were, we found ourselves in their cluttered garage, where things got a bit steamy. We didn't go *all the way* but nearly, amidst the sacks of potatoes, kids bikes and garden implements. Gasping and sweating (well, I was), Sue led me back through the adjoining door into the kitchen where, to my horror, her husband Paul was emptying crisps into dishes.

'Oh, there you are, love', he said. 'I didn't know where you were, and some people wanted nibbles'.

I nearly fainted as she replied, casually, 'Oh sorry Paul, I've been playing rudies in the garage with John.'

To my further amazement he replied, 'Have we got any peanuts?' nodding at me as I slithered past him. I learnt a lot about suburban married life during that time!

But the showstopper moment came late one night when my brother-in-law Pete and I had been 'football training' – a euphemism for a few exercises in the tiny village hall 'gym', followed by a casual trot round the village and seamlessly into the local pub for three hours, after which we staggered home and were having several more. My sister had wisely gone to bed when I drunkenly fished from my wallet the copy of my resettlement form and handed it solemnly to Pete. He read it slowly and silently, shaking his head in disbelief at its contents.

'You cheeky bastard! I'm going to write to the RAF and tell them what a useless fuggin' mechanic you are – and that you've failed the course!' The next day we told my sister Jean. She was incredulous but we all laughed about it and my two months with them was very special. I loved their village life, made a few friends and had a ball.

But all good things must come to an end and I had a little unfinished business to conclude with Her Majesty before I could continue with my rehabilitation into civilian life. (I have already told you about my hair-related setback that day in Chapter 32. Bastards!)

38.   The RAF and Me

I think it all started because my father was a pilot and although I didn't really get on with him in my teenage years, I think I always idolised him. He was my hero and I wanted to emulate him. In some ways I did, but not in flying, although in my teens in the Air Training Corps I flew a glider solo briefly (three launches) but apart from a few flights in small light aircraft and a lot of passenger air travel, I never got to fly as a pilot – perhaps one day, eh?

I had the minimum everything for qualifying to join the Royal Air Force as a pilot. I was the minimum height, the minimum weight, achieved the minimum qualifications (five hard-won 'O' levels including Maths and English Language) and I was the minimum age too, seventeen. Looking back, I had the minimum experience in life as well! At the four-day aircrew selection centre in Biggin Hill I was up against men (the maximum age was twenty-six). At an immature seventeen, I was just a boy in comparison to most of them.

Nevertheless, at the end of the four days I was told to re–apply in two years' time, not terminal news as some were told, so there was some hope. However, when asked by the selectors what I was going to do now that I had been unsuccessful, I replied I was thinking of joining anyway, on the ground side – an idea which had been slowly forming in my brain – in the very unlikely eventuality of failure.

'Good man!' was the reaction. 'With your qualifications you will do well', I was told, so back to the recruiting centre in Nottingham I went, to sit various tests – which seemed relatively easy in comparison to the officers selection board.

Amongst a whole raft of trades, I was offered an unusual one, strike photography, which apparently didn't come up very often. I often wished I had taken it, but it sounded a lonely and specialised job. It involved doing the usual RAF photographers course at the, then, most modern school of photography in Europe at RAF

Cosford (where, incidentally, I eventually ended up, although on a different course) and then going on for further specialist training. It was explained to me that the job entailed me alone loading up a photo-reconnaissance aircraft with camera and film prior to take-off and, after the flight, taking the camera and film out again and developing it; obviously highly-secret stuff.

But I just wanted to be one of the lads, as ever in my life, and discussed the considerable range of trade opportunities offered to me with Dad. I wanted to be involved with aircraft, I was mad-keen on them for four years in the Air Training Corps, so with Dad's advice about radio being a vital communication both past and present, I opted for the exotic position of *Electronic Mechanic – Air Communications*. It sounded better than it actually was, being basically a radio mechanic, but they couldn't call it that, now could they? And that was basically that. I became one and stayed one for four and a half years. Take out the six months basic and trade training, add the two months it took me to reach eighteen and start 'men's service', and I did five years and two months in the RAF, coming out at twenty-three. Incidentally, you don't find out until you've joined ANY of the services that your time doesn't start until you are eighteen; a rude shock for those who joined young and later regretted it.

Initially happy, my attitude swung fairly steadily against staying any longer than I had signed up for, after about a year. My mates on similar periods of service quickly discovered that if you wanted to get on and rise higher in the RAF you needed to become fully skilled, not half-skilled as we were. This was achieved by taking a one-year 'fitter's course', which was not possible to do on a five year contract. You needed to be signed on for at least nine years and, if you did, you immediately got an increase in pay of about a pound a week. That was a lot of money to us, then on basic pay of about six pounds a week, so everyone signed on for nine years. Everyone, that is, except me!

The reason I did not was because I went home for the weekend and talked it over in the pub with Dad. Our relationship was much better now that I had left home. For the first time in my life, I found him a very experienced man of the world with a fantastic wealth of mature advice, but only if it was sought. On that occasion he gave me a great perspective on life at a crucial time. He pointed out that even if I did sign on, there was no guarantee of a fitter's course (in fact, I was actually offered one later, but declined it). Dad's view was that a pound a week extra was not really a fortune, even if it seemed so at the time. It was not enough to tie up one's life for another four years. This proved great advice.

With unerring accuracy, as it later transpired, Dad predicted that if I came out of my existing contract at twenty three, I was still young enough to change my career and might still not be married ('Me married?' I thought at the time. 'You must be joking!'). But if I signed on for the minimum nine years, I would be twenty-seven at least when I came out, and I would probably be married and possibly have children. Dear old Dad was spot on, as it happened. I came out single – just – at twenty-three and by twenty-seven was married with two kids. But, of course, I wasn't in the RAF.

All my mates duly signed on and took the Queen's extra twenty shillings but some even had later to buy themselves out.

Bang on Dad, you were dead right!

Gradually but steadily my love for the Royal Air Force diminished, although it never did for air travel. I began to think ahead for the first time and my attitude to the RAF as a career changed fairly quickly. I realised that the longer you stayed in the services, the more 'institutionalised' you became. Pretty soon you became dependent on the forces to feed you, clothe you and put a roof over your head. Somehow, that didn't seemed right to me.

I realised I had some years to go before I could change careers and do something else, so what could I do in the meantime? Well, I have always loved travel, so I vowed to go abroad and see as much of the world as I could, courtesy of Her Majesty, and I did. Although I was based on the same South Coast RAF Station for four and a half years – a length of service in one place virtually unheard of in the RAF – I was lucky enough to travel from there to Malta, Cyprus, Gibraltar, Gan (the Maldives), Singapore, Bermuda, New York and lastly, and definitely least – Libya! Never anywhere abroad for more than three weeks, it was heaven and, being a single man, I loved it. Compared to many who served in the RAF I was very lucky to travel and see so much.

The only other avenue open to me to better myself at that time was education. I passed 'O' level Technical Drawing and History for something to do, at last amassing seven GCEs. I tried German but *it voz eine catastrophe*. Unlike the other subjects, I had to study the subject off the camp at evening class one night a week in Chichester. As an adult class, it was fast moving and I soon found being on detachment abroad for three weeks was a disaster. Because I was 'between cars' at the time, I had to catch the train to Chichester for the class. That was ok when it was on a Wednesday but soon after that the class was switched to Fridays. This was particularly difficult, as I had to catch the return train back into the village arriving about 9 pm.

Now Friday nights were booze-up nights for us, the format usually an early evening start, becoming a pub crawl through the village, ending up at the Railway Inn, our second home. Here I alighted from the train after my German class, stone-cold sober, unlike my rowdy mates, who had started drinking several hours previously. Needless to say, I was a target for much bawdy ribaldry as soon as I arrived in the pub with my books. Every single time they would disappear and I would have to find them again, in such places as the gents, once even in the ladies, above the cistern. My attempt at learning German did not last long.

As I got past two and then three years of my five years' service, I began to look ahead and wonder what I was going to do upon my re-entry into the real world of civilian life as a 23-year-old. As dear old Dad had had a good life in the selling profession, I wondered whether I could emulate him, eventually becoming a manager, a leader of men. Dad was an area sales manager with a national company and had earned a sound reputation as a good manager. His career would have gone a lot further but for the considerable deafness that plagued him for most of his adult life (the deafness I inherited – eh?).

The Air Force had various schemes for 'resettlement' and various careers guidance officers to advise. When I first broached going into selling the officer shook his head and said this was unwise. As I had over the minimum five 'O' levels, why didn't I go into 'safe, secure' careers, such as banking, teaching or the Civil Service? Although I still wanted to go into selling (and did finally, and loved it) I allowed the RAF to fix me up with an interview at a teacher training college sympathetic to 'ex-regulars'. Everything went wrong on the day. I was an hour and a half late, it was a poor interview and I was offered a place! I turned it down but often wondered what would have happened if I had taken it. No idea!

So at last the great day came and I was released back into society after five years, one month and six days – not that I was counting! Looking back, I am grateful, I had a ball, as I hope is portrayed in this book. I always wanted to write it all down as I remembered it, to see if I could convey the funny side of it, because it was mostly a scream to me at the time. I really enjoyed myself and although I'm sure I had down times, I really can't remember many. I like to think that the RAF took me from boy to man and although I certainly wasn't the complete finished article when I left, the experience of mixing with so many other men from different backgrounds was a great leveller for life. It certainly knocked my rough edges off – and I had a few to be sure!

The most important thing I learned was how to get on with my fellow man. Pity there weren't more women around but you can't have everything! There is no other way to learn, you just have to mix, live, eat, breathe and sleep very close to others. Snorers, belchers, farters, boozers, halitosis sufferers, smokers, scratchers, flashers, masturbators, fat slobs, thin slobs, lanky gits and short-arses – in five years I came across them all. Although there were one or two real arseholes, I don't think I ever lived alongside any individual I really hated. There were a few I didn't particularly like being around but the 'melting-pot' syndrome is generally good for building tolerance in the long term.

As I write this in 2010 there seems to be so much intolerance amongst one's fellow human beings, be it with neighbours, colleagues, authority or whoever. I count myself fortunate to have escaped a lot of that due, I believe, to the five years of my life I invested in the Royal Air Force.

Put simply, I wouldn't have missed it for the world.

Thanks for listening!

~ END ~